The Ocean Fell Into the Drop

The Ocean Fell Into the Drop

TERENCE STAMP

Published by Repeater Books
An imprint of Watkins Media Ltd
19-21 Cecil Court
London
WC2N 4EZ
UK

www.repeaterbooks.com

A Repeater Books paperback original 2017
1

Distributed in the United States by Random House, Inc.,
New York.

Cover design: Johnny Bull/Francis Bacon

Typefaces: Garamond/Frutiger

ISBN: 978-1-910924-53-2

Ebook ISBN: 978-1-910924-54-9

Printed and bound in the United Kingdom

"I've worked for Pinter and Stoppard, I'd be happy to work with you."

Thank you, Lois Stein

FOREWORD

Just in case you have wandered into one of my favourite booksellers (they all are) and this carefully bound volume is in your hand: before you fork out your hard-earned cash, let's be clear about its content.

One of the early blessings in my life was the clarity regarding my path through it, courtesy of Gary Cooper; it was to be an artist in the arts. As I am closer to the end of life than the beginning, these are the recollections I am hoping to relate to other creative artists in the busy, tough world out there.

I have a bright nephew who has inherited the looks and street smarts of his grandfather, my Dad. He is one of the future stars in London's great City, and he told me categorically that 98% of the world's wealth is owned by 0.1% of the population. This fact is so overwhelming it does look like there is nothing the individual can actually do about it.

Yet recently, at one of his appearances, the Dalai Lama was asked: 'What can we do about the crazy havoc in which we live?' His terse reply was, 'Attend to the crazy havoc inside yourself first.'

Coincidentally, in the land of the lakes where they really appreciate the value of cash, the Swiss have completed a 17-mile underground Collider circuit beneath their borders with France at a cost of $4.4 billion, where they bombard 115 billion protons every nanosecond at the speed of light, in anticipation of finding a semi-mythical particle whose status implies a world of hidden dimensions. $4.4 billion. One wonders what value Alan Turing would have put on the man-machine. Yet as a gentleman and poet once wrote, 'If a leaf on a green tree turned red, the whole tree is changed.'

Ego vir: pars verissima esse myta bilia,
sed ominia sunt beterna mutato; obstretat.

1

In the beginning was the word, and the word was Hu. It would probably be more accurate to say in the beginning was the sound, as it was the sound about them, the wind, the bird in flight, and later in the tolling of bells, that the ancients called Hu: it meant divine. In Sanskrit the word man represented mind, so the early humans considered themselves divine minds.

All Tom's kids inherited bits of his DNA in the looks department

Growing up I had little contact with the divine mind that was my father, as he was at sea stoking the coal fires that propelled the merchant ships in the Second World War. Whilst I was lucky enough to inherit Tom Stamp's bone structure, the earliest conscious male influence was from Gary Cooper. My mother was an inveterate moviegoer, yet deprived of this pleasure by my arrival apparently decided she couldn't miss Coop's latest, and I was trundled alongside her, aged three years and six months, to the Old Grand in nearby Barking Road, E13. The film: *Beau Geste*. A saga in the desert with Cooper as a legionnaire. Was it destiny or luck that my initial experience of the silver screen exposed me to the peerless Cooper?

Both, is how I view it today. One of the most handsome men God ever put breath into had the profoundest effect on me. The feelings released in me sitting in the dark of the one-shilling-and-ninepenny seats was to set the course of my life. The timeless part of him he gave to the camera reached into me as if there was no separation. The desire to be like him, initially a legionnaire, and later an actor, matured as I grew, remained my secret. A secret kept for sixteen years, when our first telly arrived.

My Mum packed me off to school prematurely when I was three, but this was later reprieved until I was five. However, although the primary school was a really nice modern building, the area we had located to from Bow, Plaistow, was quite middle class when it was invaded by the hordes trying to evade the bombing of the East India docks; yet the actual method of teaching us five to ten year-olds was mostly learning-by-rote, to which my particular brain wasn't suited. The contrary, in fact. Of course, this led most of the teachers to consider me a dunce. This fortunately was offset by the fact that lots of the other boy and girl pupils did seek me out on Mondays to enquire how I had spent the weekend.

My Mum, unlike my instructors, had no such doubts. Her eldest had her complete faith. She would bolster my introversion yet counter my shyness with her own philosophy. I recall her once asking me what I wanted to do with my life. I guess I was about eleven or twelve and had miraculously passed the eleven-plus.

John Stamp, my younger brother, with the Irish side of our tribe in the hop fields

Never dreaming of sharing my innermost aspiration, I asked her what she would have become given the opportunities.

'Something there is only one of … like a Pope.'

It never actually occurred to me just how poverty-stricken we were until I started being invited into other boys' houses and I noticed they had carpet on the floors. I don't recall anyone outside of the family being invited indoors. It later emerged my mother was ashamed by our furnishings, or lack of them. She counteracted this by ensuring we were always spotless and as well turned-out as possible. This probably was the reason later in life I was included in the Best Dressed Man in best-of-Britain lists.

When my mother passed away and I was spurred to scribble an autobiography, some of the girls I had attended Plaistow Grammar School with contacted me. They all agreed they hadn't considered how hard-up we were as I was always so smart and clean.

Chadwin Road housed the roughest kids in the neighbourhood: the cheapest always does. None of us were truly content there. A bit like those seats in the new buses that faced backwards, artistically designed to make you feel nauseous. There was much to be said for Plaistow. It had an open air lido at our end of the Beckton Road Park, the park where it was claimed seven winds blew; fact or not, it must have extended the direction of the fine aspects of my breath. A library in Prince Regent's Lane where I initially went with my Mum, and later under my own

Chris and Terry before sibling rivalry

steam came upon Edgar Wallace's *Four Just Men* who dwelt in Curzon Street. And lastly 'the dumps', a barren mass of accumulated rubbish that stretched endlessly beyond Tolgate Primary School's grounds in the 'rec', a haphazard training ground and football pitch. I mention these as the great pastime that became an integral part of my childhood: roaming. Broadening my outlook like Columbus, 'the less we knew where we were the farther we roamed'. It built my very fussy appetite for the cooked meals, usually three a day, that miraculously manifested with my Mum's share of my Dad's £12-a-week wages.

Ethel Esther Perrott, to give my Mum her name before she met Tom Stamp, was highly intuitive, and she developed this trait by accepting it. 'The more I trust it, it trusts me', she once told me. She never allowed her children to have a dummy to suck, as she didn't want them to become reliant on a 'thing'. Self-reliance was her intention for us. Later she told me: 'Newborns are one hundred percent receptive, the first impressions are the deepest'. Another example: if I either scalded or burned my fingers, she instructed me to blow on them and, when I confessed I was frequently unnerved at school by exams and the like, she coached me into taking a couple of deep breaths whenever the fears surfaced. I increased this to three as it felt better. Numerology was still a long way off and didn't come into my life until my initial foray to the East.

These sessions with Mum had a different tone than the everyday tips: 'Don't go out in the cold with wet hair'. It was as though, particularly when he came home from the war, that my Dad observed (he was a serious observer) his wife's influence on his son and decided I was already a sissy, that our communication continued as though he wasn't there. Ethel being aware of this, took my upbringing on her own considerable shoulders.

Lessons in life became lessons for life as her tone of voice left no doubt, subtle as it was.

The intelligence of my Mum manifested early. She had passed the toughest examinations that would have enabled her to go to any of the foremost schools in the Bow-Stepney districts, but her Dad, Alf Perrott, would have none of it. He didn't want her 'getting above herself', i.e. believing she was better than her parents. Deprived of the chance to an education worthy of her ability, she went to a low-grade institution that she hated. Leaving at fourteen, she applied for and received an apprenticeship as a typewriter

Cool is born

mechanic in Holborn, and in a year she had mastered everything necessary to completely dismantle and reassemble a typewriter.

This early frustration in her own life manifested in the desire for all her kids to achieve the best education out there.

I discovered recently that she gave an astonishing performance of Rosalind in the school's production of *As You Like It*. So it must have given her profound satisfaction when all her children passed the eleven-plus.

The first landmark of my youth occurred when I passed the eleven-plus, the anticipation of which had condemned me to months of thought-fear, no small part of which were the hopes of the two entrenched working-class families, hopes unexpressed yet felt, by yours truly, the next generation.

The eleven-plus, or scholarship as we called it, was divided into three papers: Maths, English and General Knowledge. The Maths paper was returned blank, save my name neatly underlined. The second, similar. It was only the General Knowledge exam I responded to. Questions like, "Draw how the letter E would look reflected in a mirror", must have caught the eye of a fellow left-handed, right-brain-dominated examiner.

It was obvious I didn't possess the musical talents of my mother, yet on winter evenings we would listen to our valve wireless together and I never thought about the fact it was mainly classical seeds that were sown that sprouted in later life. Mario Lanza's impeccable renderings often connect me to those wirelines times as I am moved in ways I'm sure you're all familiar with. In this early listening with one ear close to the failing valves deep parts of me were touched, later allowing me to understand I was to become my instrument. At the time I was just jealous of chum David Taylor who played trombone. As an only child, he was given whatever he wanted. Like only sons I've consequently come across, he lived in his own universe.

Me with Granny Kate Perrott

Getting the navy-blue blazer with the Plaistow County Grammar badge on the pocket and attending the school building in Prince Regent's Lane was reassuring to my teenage self-esteem. A great compliment to the architect of the day, unlike the concrete erections of today's barracks and the majority of public buildings developers favour. Until midway through the first term when I realised even the elegant grammar school with its own playing field was beholden to the learning-by-rote system which pervaded all its disciplines with the exception of art and music. Depression set in. My two brothers, Christopher Thomas and Richard Francis, were now on the scene and the little two-up two-down at 124 was less than peaceful. I took to going to my granny Kate's house. She still lived in Barking

Road, where we'd all lived after the initial move from Canal Road, Bow. On her rug on the floor in front of her coal-fire in the supportive quiet of her presence was where I attempted my homework, while she made me a marmalade sandwich. I recall going every day during the summer holidays, drawing and painting a scene from the Beckton Lido in an effort to impress the beautiful auburn-haired Miss Fowler, the only teacher I really took to.

Certain conditions happened in my teenage life which at the time seemed unwarranted and certainly uncalled for, and which at the time I bitterly resented, which just goes to show. This particular event I often have cause to recall, and its momentous ramifications down the line, the District Line, as it happens, as I often pass the station Bromley-by-Bow where the underground surfaces on its

Our sister Lynette, brother Richard and brother John

route eastwards and where the St Andrew's Hospital once stood, where so much attention was focused on my feet, or "plates of meat" as my Dad called them. As a boy my Dad was often forced to go barefoot as his mother pawned her kids' shoes, shoes their Dad had bought them in his time at home from sea. Mary Allen Stamp contributed the Irish storytelling blood to our family and had a liking for the sherbet, always an expensive habit, even in those days. It was because of this humiliation, to say nothing of the physical discomfort, that my Dad was so aware of his footwear, a trait I inherited in spades; the desire to be well shod.

It began one morning as I grounded my tootsies on getting out of bed. What was this pain, so severe every morning and not much better during the day? I was taken on the first Saturday to see Dr Brandreth in his surgery in the shadow of the Farraday School, an impressive Victorian heap which I had avoided by winning the scholarship. The doctor noted my recent spurt in height and diagnosed 'fallen arches', a common response the feet have to accommodate the sudden change in equilibrium. I was given a letter and ordered to report to St Andrew's Hospital, where I stumbled into their orthopaedic department. (If the British Health Service is as good today as it was in the Fifties, I can see why it's the envy of the world.)

I was reassured my condition was normal and soon remedied. The specialist pointed out that my right foot was a half-size bigger than my left. I was advised to favour the larger when buying shoes. Until I could afford to have my footwear made-to-measure (What!).

A nurse then escorted me to an electrical device, put an inch of water into two footbaths, connected two metal plates to the machine and placed them in the water, one under each foot. A pleasant charge reverberated through my feet, sometimes lifting them clear out of the water. The treatment was timed for ten minutes. I was told to come every day. It was only a few stops on the District Line – Plaistow, West Ham, Bromley. I would go directly after school. I became so familiar with the routine that I could assemble the electrodes myself. I would sometimes be well into my ten minutes before anyone spotted me. It was a chore, yet the pain soon stopped. And as I said before, the ramifications, albeit years later, were life-changing. The therapist instructed me in a specific foot stretching exercise, which I do to this day. 'You don't want your feet, your contact with the earth, stopping you growing to six foot, do you?'

'You think I will be tall?'

'That's what your feet tell me'. He gave my tootsies a congratulatory squeeze. 'Noble feet', he added. 'Take care of them, they'll carry you well.'

It was probably this early focus of attention on what it was that I actually stood upon that imbued me with what my relatives called a foot fetish. And it's not untrue that I began to notice what footwear other boys, and later men, wore. We were a bit pushed to buy any gear and our footwear came from a house off the Cumberland Road whose front room had been transformed to accommodate hundreds of boxes of shoes. No one ever asked where these brand new and stylish footwear came from, yet they were affordable and available. It's encouraging to see how well a lot of the male populace are shod with the kind of shoes I never even aspired to until I met the great George Cleverley. I rarely consider the attire of men whose feet connect to the earth with 'trainers'.

Mum always made sure we were spick-and-span when we went out, and this extended to underwear. A trait that only became enhanced when

John Drew, Terence Henry and Christopher Thomas

I started to meet the ladies. More than one told me most women paid attention to what undergarments men wore. So, being an optimist about the fairer sex, I never left home underdressed, as I never knew when an unexpected, seemingly spontaneous striptease might be on the cards.

Later on in life, my brother Chris offered finite advice on the subject of the availability of the ladies when he expressed his philosophy: 'Always try, you'd be surprised how many are up for it.' Since his change of cosmic address, many women have told me they considered Chris a dangerous man to be alone with. I've been told by happily settled ones that they were made to confront their unexpressed desires and lack of passion in night-to-night life.

2

"It works in practice but does it work in theory?"

- Overheard on a French subway

I didn't come across girls my own age who found me attractive, and it wasn't until I started work that older women seemed to pick up on me. As I matured, these encounters with mature women stood me in good stead with girls my own age. Once at Plaistow Grammar I tried out for school plays without much success. I began to feel my secret dream would not be realised, so I tried another direction and auditioned for an amateur drama club who were casting Somerset Maugham's *The Sacred Flame*. I was thrilled to get a part, albeit the part of a sixty year-old, but it was a lead and I gave no thought to the fact that leading parts have endless lines to commit to memory. The result was I trod the boards of the East Ham Town Hall theatre and my performance, such as it was, consisted of stumbling through my big speeches. In truth, I may very well have opted for another livelihood had not my Mum and Dad, mainly Mum, forked out for a television set which became the honorary guest in our cosy living room.

The impact of the television was exciting, yet it didn't take long to realise having a black-and-white picture actually in one's home wasn't comparable to the feeling of being in a cinema. That moment when the house lights dim and one's individuality is given up to merge with the collective and the empathy with one's favourite performers is kindled deep inside.

By this time, I had seen never-to-be-forgotten Gene Tierney and Tyrone Power in Maugham's *The Razor's Edge*. Afterwards retrieving the book at the Beckton Road Library. Naturally I was in love with the exquisite Tierney. (Many years later I got a date with her but she didn't show.)

I had also seen Cary Grant in *The Bishop's Wife*, and when I discovered he'd been born Archie Leech and was a working-class lad from Bristol, I was impressed in ways it's hard to explain. I didn't stop watching television, yet the artists with their 'proper' accents, as we called them, didn't strike any lasting chords. I started thinking, 'I could do better than that'. As time passed these notions became vocal. My Dad wore it the first few times, but when I persisted he looked me straight on and said:

'Son, people like us don't do things like that.'

I opened my mouth to express my view, but he continued.

'Son, I don't want you to talk about it anymore.'

Looking back to that altercation in the tiny living room in Cladwin Road, that could very well have been the end of my dream. Expressed, albeit obliquely, for the very first time, it could have been shattered by my father's firm opposition. The curious thing was it strengthened my resolve. Knowing the implications of going against my Dad's rarely expressed house rules, the realisation came that I would have to leave home.

There wasn't a single soul I could seek advice from. No boy left home other than to get married, even then most of them just moved into the spare room upstairs with their betrothed. I was compelled to just bide my time. What I needed was a motion of the universe.

However, I left Fairbairn House, the boys club I belonged to. The warden, both the power and money behind the enterprise, Sir Ian Horobin, had taken an unreturned interest in me. It was said he'd been in a Japanese prison in the war and was presently the Conservative Member of Parliament for Oldham. I don't know how true this is, but he was the only man I had ever met who wore a pince-nez perched on the bridge of his nose. Farley Granger he wasn't.

I joined the YMCA in Prince Regent's Lane and took up table-tennis, got into the club's team, and began meeting boys a little older than myself yet more than a little talented. Ray Dorkin was the best junior player in Britain and Bobby Raybold had had his backhand smash taught to him by Viktor Barna, whose own backhand attack had made him a world champion. You could say he was the Roger Federer of the day, albeit on a table court. I believe Socrates said, 'First is beauty, victory is secondary', the aforementioned were appropriate examples.

If I'd lived to be a hundred I would never have been able to play like Ray or Bobby, yet I did accompany them to tournaments where I met some memorable athletic girls. Ray even knew the Rowe twins who headed the English team for which he played as the junior representative. I had no sooner left school, where I had failed all my GCEs yet secured employment in an advertising agency. I told them I had passed all eight. I was given to believe my job was a learner copywriter, but it was in fact messenger-filing clerk. I guess the law-of-like-kinds brought us together.

In the Fifties, the dreaded National Service rested heavily on teenage boys. Two years of incarceration and learning to kill, albeit with a short haircut. I've always had trouble killing anything, even before I became a vegetarian, and slowly the idea dawned upon me that if I could avoid my military service completely I could leave home and use the two years, which my contemporaries didn't have, to try to make a reality of my dream. If it all came to nothing I could return to a more conventional lifestyle with no time lost and maybe a few more arrows to my bow. I started to privately mimic the posh accents on TV.

One Saturday Ray Dorkin took me with him to meet a chum of his who lived behind the Pronto Cleaners opposite the Granada Cinema in East Ham, and that was where I first encountered David Baxter, who was to affect the direction of my life. I heard it said that David resembled Russ Tamblyn, the American actor, yet Dave was his own man, an original and not like anyone I had ever met. We got on instantly and it was he who recited something he'd read. Words to the effect that if a leaf on a green tree turns red the whole tree is changed. Even at that time it made sense to me, as it implied using one's time and energy to bring about change in oneself rather than try to alter others. I had no way of knowing how long I would plough this furrow and endure the loneliness entailed in doing the opposite of nearly everyone else.

Wanstead always represented to me the well-to-do end of East London living, and I got to know the upper-class neighbourhood well when I worked as an assistant golfer at Wanstead Golf Club part-time, evenings and weekends, during my final years at Plaistow Grammar.

3

Knit faster with Knitmaster

The two years at work in advertising seemed to have flashed by, and I was summoned to attend my National Service medical the first Friday after my eighteenth birthday in a public building just past the underground station – it was the only time I wasn't looking forward to getting the bus and sitting upstairs as it passed through Wanstead Park and Flats as I hadn't been able to come up with a single idea of how the dreaded time in khaki could be gotten out of.

There were half a dozen fellas like myself being supervised by a few doctors. Pulses taken, heartbeats measured, weighed and for me an exciting height measurement. Which didn't happen that often. 'Six foot', the measurer announced. Six feet! A long-standing personal ambition I had evidently achieved without notice. I was given a couple of sheets of paper and a pen to answer all the questions concerning my health. Of course I entered my tonsil and appendix extractions but I couldn't find any other potential negatives in the questionnaire. I hadn't given a thought to how healthy I was. The final question just asked for 'Any other conditions', with a sizeable space for answers. At that moment the lengthy treatment I had had at the St Andrew's Hospital came to mind. I looked around, all the other boys had their heads down, so I filled in what I could remember about the fallen arches.

My paper was collected. Several of the health assessors studied our answers and then one of them called my name. I followed him into a little room and sat down opposite him. My paper was on the desk in front of him.

'Fallen arches?' he asked. 'Tell me about that.'

I did, doing my best to appear nonchalant yet giving full details of my daily forays when I got to the practice I'd been instructed to follow. I slipped off my shoes. I was into casuals at the time without socks. I was intending to get my legs sunburnt but July hadn't been sunny. My feet looked exposed and pink. Anyway, making sure he could see, I lifted my left heel and right toes, and reversed right heel left toes. I did several repetitions and explained how I could also shuffle my feet over a broomstick handle if he had one handy. He held up his hand. I thought I'd overdone it.

'And did the morning pains cease?'

'Oh, yes.'

'After how long?'

'Oh, six, seven months.'

He marked the top of the questionnaire. I could read the Roman numerals upside down: III. 'When do I expect to be called up?' I asked.

'Oh, you won't be called up. I'm afraid you're not fit enough. I'm sorry.'

I did my best to look downcast. Once clear of the building I let my feelings overwhelm me. I sat down at the bus stop on the heath. I could feel the air entering my nostrils, the sun on my face, the buses I let pass seemed a brighter red than usual. There was a stillness of my brain which the chirruping of the birds didn't disturb, inside me it was quiet yet aware.

Later in life when studying Sufism I came across the symbolism for the days of the week and discovered Friday was the day of prayers answered and dreams realised, and that Friday at Wanstead bus stop came instantly to mind.

When I arrived home after the timeless moments in Wanstead, my Mum and Dad were indoors and keen to know what had occurred.

'Looks like I'm not doing it', I said. 'Not fit enough.'

Mum's reaction was unexpected.

'What's not fit with you?'

I certainly didn't want her complaining to any officials.

'The fallen arches', I reminded her. 'The daily sessions at St Andrew's. I had to tell them, they needed to know everything.'

'You don't seem concerned.'

'Concerned. Are you kidding? Two years of my life learning about guns. How to wound and kill people.'

Dad interjected. 'Would have made a man of you.'

It sounded like he'd been rather hoping to get me out of the house for a year or two. I made a mental note.

'What's for dinner?' I asked, intending to close the subject on an amicable note.

The dreams for my life had remained unsaid, deep in my heart, so it was overcoming a kind of reserve that I met David Baxter at the newly opened Milk Bar on Greengate corner to share my good fortune and confess my long-held plan, which I couldn't quite believe a road was being opened to. Baxter was obviously supportive. He'd done his stint and felt it was a complete waste of a dynamic moment in his life.

'Listen', he confided leaning closer over his milkshake. 'I've heard about an outfit that is teaching Method acting. It's evening classes and is modelled on the Stanislavsky Method they teach in New York, where Brando studied.' Our mutual new hero. 'You would like to study it yourself?' I asked.

'Oh yeah. I mean if nothing ever comes of it, it's got to have benefits in anything you do. If we take it, we could share a flat up West. I mean nothing is happening around here.'

And so it began.

4

Beginning in the basement, yet a step up from E13

64 Harley Street had a basement. The rent was £24 a month. I remember the figure because the £8 a month that I received from the scholarship I was awarded from the Webber-Douglas Dramatic Academy only paid my share of the rent. Baxter had been befriended by a fellow would-be actor named George Martin and he became the third flat mate for our basement quarters. The overriding memory I have of my drama school days was being hungry – the cash I had been able to put away from my advertising job soon went and the word amongst the girls at Webber

The first real star in my orbit, Chita Riveira

that I was anybody's for a bowl of soup and a croissant wasn't true, yet it wasn't completely untrue either. I found a job backstage at Her Majesty's Theatre where Leonard Bernstein's *West Side Story* had recently opened. Although I was only working a carbon-arc (a follow-spot) from the back of the gallery, I did get to witness Chita Rivera seven times a week, the first performer I'd seen in the flesh who could sing, dance and act. It was an honour to illuminate her talent so frequently and I must confess I was inspired by her.

How often has one heard, 'Oh it's in the stars' or 'It is written'? The fact is one only knows by what happens as it happens. Having said this, what actually occurred in my life was that when I made the decision to follow my dream it was the most difficult I'd ever had to make, going against my father's belief and my mother's emotional wishes, considerable, to keep me at home. However, once I had actually cut loose there was a big tidal change.

It was a miracle that I was awarded the only scholarship given at any of the leading London drama schools, and the schooling that followed before that fateful evening when the agent James Fraser caught my only performance of Shakespeare's Iago. My first teacher of voice at the Webber-Douglas was the unforgettable Kathryn Fleming, who just happened to possess the most wonderful voice I'd ever heard. In improving my voice I was compelled to address my innermost fears head-on, as this was tantamount of discovering my inner voice; the audible testament to one's essence or the energy one is born with. Kathy was the perfect guide for this voyage I'd taken, which only came fully to light when she told me that not only did she herself come from London's East End, but a road barely past the Beckton Road Library, the first rungs of my literary ladder, where she still lived with her mother. With renewed efforts I followed her guidance. Curiously, the actual breathing was never discussed directly, yet in straddling the extended verses of the classics and holding a single thought entailed in the recitation of a sonnet, the breath and its inbuilt rhythms were being energised almost without my knowledge.

Kathy Fleming was my morning star.

The system at Webber was to have students feature in three or four plays every term. Some leads, some supporting. Besides giving us a wide variety of roles, it would prepare us for the arduousness of weekly repertory, where most of us would get our initial jobs, if lucky.

The first Shakespeare production found me playing Lysander in A *Midsummer Night's Dream*, just right to get me started. Yet what I think of as my real initiation was the role of Iago in *Othello*, to be directed by an extremely talented Peter Buckley. As I was not familiar with the play I was hungry for direction, but the more I studied and learned my part I was consumed by the text itself, which I would often get to read between my follow-spot cues behind the Gods at Her Majesty's Theatre to the ever-inspiring live music of Leonard Bernstein's *West Side Story*.

The soliloquies that Iago delivers directly to the audience, in which he gives vent to his rageful revenge, leave the spectator in no doubt as to the depth of his innate evil. At some point in my work on these soliloquies I came upon the notion that in the prospect of actually baring his deepest desires, bringing them into the open, he could rouse himself to orgasm. I decided to save this revelation for the evening of my sole performance at the Chanticleer Theatre.

The other director, as clear in my memory as he was all those years ago, was the actor Moray Watson. Apart from Moray being a charming, urbane guy, he was a professional actor actually playing in the West End. In truth, he was only ten years older than me, but he was so mature, so far along in the business, that it could have been double the years between us. I had been cast as the Earl of Harpenden in Terence Rattigan's *While the Sun Shines*. It was a role so far from me that I felt intimidated by the other students also in the cast. Moray intuitively sensed this and went to some lengths to reassure me, even giving me a ticket to see him at work one evening in the play he was in, *The Grass is Greener* by Hugh and Margaret Williams. He was outstanding in his role of the butler, even creating a nervous tic with his hands, which had the audience laughing throughout the evening.

Yet one rehearsal at Webber has stayed with me. There was a delivery by my character of simply the word 'Yes', repeated three times, which I just didn't know what to do with. Seeing this, Moray stepped toward me and said:

'Do it like this.'

I now know that ninety-nine times out of a hundred it was the wrong way to direct an actor, yet with his adroitness of mind he simply stepped across the stage area repeating the 'Yesses' at leisure, the delivery so differently and seemingly spontaneous that I knew I was in the presence of a master of light comedy. Now, I knew immediately there was no way I could emulate him, yet with those words he conveyed all the magic of comedy: the timing itself was the magic.

On reflection came the realisation that the chasm between Morey's mastery of comic timing and my lack of it could be viewed, or rather reduced to, one distinction: his timing was second nature.

It was no use being in denial when faced with this fact, yet the only positive route open to me was to make a start, however minimal. I set about incorporating, or rather experimenting, with timing in the everyday conversations I had. One of the first things I became aware of was my own Dad's timing. When he decided to speak it meant he invariably got a laugh.

The Sunday lunch following my decision, my family were assembled, and our Mum was relating a story about her married sister, who had embarked on an affair. The gentleman in question was of a certain age and had trouble with a complete performance, so he had apparently initially satisfied our aunt orally. Of course we siblings were relishing this hot gossip, yet our Dad was curdling with embarrassment. Yet Mum, making the most of the moment, elaborated on the story; recently the lover had been roused to a complete erection and came for the first time in years. This revelation was followed by a reverential quiet, into which our Dad commented, 'Blimey. It must have come out in lumps.'

The timing of this one-liner was so memorable that forever after the boyfriend was known only as Lumpy.

The lasting gift that Moray laid on me was that once out of school and into the profession, he continued to take me to supper after his show, to the wonderful Seven Stars restaurant upstairs at Lyons Corner House where we would tell each other, or rather he would tell me, inside showbiz tales. Apparently my hero Cary Grant was extremely 'careful' with money, yet Moray never let on about how Mr Grant explained away his 'borrowing' of his clever 'business gesture'. He did tell me that when he asked Cary when he was going to retire, his answer was, 'When I no longer get the gal'.

These suppers at the Steven Stars helped to bridge feeling like a student to embracing the role of working actor.

Cary Grant went to *The Grass is Greener* and agreed to star in the film. He insisted Moray play his butler and 'borrowed' his play of moving his hands, which you can see in the film today.

Moray Watson, my evening star.

Anthony Newley was another guiding light in my chosen path. His

Peter Ustinov, Lesley Caron and yours truly

Tom and Ethel at the premiere of *Billy Budd*

performance as the Artful Dodger in the David Lean film of *Oliver Twist* made an indelible impression on me. I was even more impressed when I learned just how he landed the role.

Being born into a poor London family and knowing a showbiz career was his destiny, he auditioned for an acting school for kids. Everyone was impressed by his ability and as his parents could not afford the academy's fees, it was agreed that he would earn his tuition by doing odd jobs, whatever needed to be done.

In his search for the young members of his cast, Lean visited the school and saw all the young would-be performers. No one caught his eye. Agreeing to have a cup of tea with the principal, he was relaxing with the staff when in came the young Newley, whirling the tray of refreshments he'd been told to make. 'Anyone for China Lee, then?' he asked.

The year on-the-boards since James Fraser had pulled me out of Webber-Douglas had passed quickly, with me playing weekly shows in what seemed like all the number one theatres in Britain, with some number two's and number three's, I may add. I was back in London rehearsing the lead in a play by John McGrath called *Why the Chicken* being directed by Lionel Bart, when I received a phonecall from my agent to go to meet Peter Ustinov, who was casting a new film he was to direct, *Billy Budd*. I knew of Melville's masterwork, having heard about the opera.

'What's the part?' I asked.

'It's for Billy', Jimmy replied.

'Blimey', I said. 'He must be desperate. Billy's a sort of angel.'

'He is; he's seen every actor in town. Now just get along to Bob Lennard's office at ABC in Golden Square. You're expected at six o'clock.'

Golden Square, I thought, that's a good omen, although I couldn't for the life of me think why.

Lionel was OK to let me off early to enable me to get to the meeting at ABC. As it happened, the British Cinema's production company wasn't actually in Golden Square, but a street leading to it. The gold was all in the energy of the amiable genius that was Peter Ustinov, a man whose presence was so formidable I felt squashed in the small, second-floor room where I encountered him and Robert Lennard, ABC's casting chief. So much so that whenever Ustinov asked me a question I was too intimidated to answer fully. It turned out to be one of these fateful occurrences that encouraged Ustinov to take me a step further: a screen test. I later discovered that one of the characteristics he was looking for in Billy was the inability to speak when facing certain situations. The Elstree screen test was successful. Ustinov's wife Suzanne later confided to me that she advised her husband, "Ee is the one.'

A few days before I was due to fly to Alicante for the six weeks of the location shoot, Lionel asked me if I'd like to meet Anthony Newley, who he was going to see. Would I!

We drove to Newley's apartment in Lionel's convertible Mercedes 220S. Lionel was a great one for the slick motor.

As soon as we arrived, the best Artful Dodger gave the creator of *Oliver*, the musical, a big hug. He'd just finished writing his first musical, *Stop the World I Want to Get Off*, and was so fired up about Lionel hearing it I don't think he even noticed I was trailing along. It was obvious how important it was for Newley to have Lionel hear his creation as he sat down at the piano and played all the songs for us (for Lionel). On reflection, Lionel Bart must have been a giant figure to Newley, a fellow East Ender, born in Bow and in keeping with Noel Coward who created both music and lyrics.

I can go on record as one of the early audiences to be thrilled by Newley and Bricusse's groundbreaking musicals … When the great one-man show of playing and singing finished, there was a breath-gaining silence, at the end of which Newley, it seemed to me, realised I was also in the room. He examined my overwhelmed face. Lionel quickly introduced me.

'This is my chum Terence. We've been working together. He's going off next week to star in Ustinov's next film.' Newley and I squarely exchanged what felt like a long look. I heard my voice address an idol. 'What to do?' I asked.

There was a lengthy silence. I can only assume Newley, being the hyper-sensitive creative artist, was giving my question the full attention of his considerable knowledge. Finally, he said: 'If in doubt, do nothing.'

On the drive back to Lionel's pad in Reece Mews, where his next door neighbour was Francis Bacon, we had the top down and the radio on. The composer of 'Fings Ain't Wot They Used to Be' was tuned in to Holst's 'Venus, the Bringer of Joy'.

Not only to have known Peter Ustinov, but to have been selected by him to play the title role in a film for which he wrote the screenplay, produced, directed and starred in, was one of the best experiences of my life. The cast included Robert Ryan, Melvin Douglas and a configuration of the finest actors in the business. The six-week location in Spain, at sea in a tall ship surrounded by this cast and crew, was the greatest debut experience a young performer could wish for. Lastly, being closely directed by such a remarkable, authentic man was like being in heaven at sea.

I never saw or heard an occasion when Peter was harsh or short with anyone. He was able to make time for everyone, most of whom left their moment smiling. I must confess I can only recall having a couple of difficulties for the whole shoot.

Robert Krasker was the director of photography, a real Turner of light. He'd lit *The Third Man*, held as 'the' example of black-and-white photography. In this regard I believe he'd suggested to the director that my dark hair should be dyed blonde. I endured four hours of peroxide, yet it was worth it, as I will explain later. His lighting plan was my first hurdle, as I could hardly keep my eyes open once under the intensity of Krasker, sunlight, carbon arcs and reflector boards. He had me face the full intensity of his lighting with closed eyes, only opening them on 'Action'. He advised me never to wear sunglass as they would weaken my eyes' resistance to light. I have followed his advice to this day.

The other worry was a direction I lit upon in Ustinov's screenplay near the end of the piece:

244 THE NOOSE IS PUT AROUND BILLY'S NECK.
245 A SERIES OF SHOTS DEPICTING THE MEN'S AGONY,
AND YET RESPECT FOR BILLY'S AGONY.

I've heard that Confucius once advised, 'Whatever you don't want to happen to you, don't do to anyone else.'

Now I'm not sure that Peter Ustinov even knew of the quote, yet he seemed to me to be a living and breathing example of it. He was unusually pliable and soft for a large man of even larger abilities. He was always open to everyone and no one was made to feel small, and as I said before he could make a laugh out of anything. When explained to me early in the shoot that he would rather I didn't attend the rushes, shown every few days, what he actually said was that my performance was exactly what he'd hoped for and that as this was my very first outing on film it was completely normal for me only to see myself during the rushes, and this he felt could disturb or alter my characterisation. Of course I didn't go to see any of the rushes at all. Yet hearing him refer to my performance after only a few days into the shoot gave me an inner confidence that somehow he didn't need my own creativity to be impinged upon. Consequently I decided I just wouldn't ask him for any direction and that if he wanted something specific he would tell me.

It was all working out fine. I was surrounded by the best actors there were and I was intuitively grading my acting to them. The great Robert Ryan never communicated with me after the press launch at the Savoy Hotel and this, whilst it felt odd at the start, was the best thing he could have done for me.

This independent line I had chosen was working out well, except that the direction in the script near the end of the film began increasingly to bother me. If Billy was at peace in the face of death, this would command the men's respect. How could one convey serenity? In the evenings in our rooms, my fellow artists relaxed by having a few drinks after work, but I didn't drink so most of my free time was spent alone. Looking back, I can see now that my particular kind of creativity was always going to entail time spent alone, yet my understanding of the word would change as time passed. I reviewed my initial introduction to professional performance and the techniques I had studied in Method acting, most days going back in my mind in an effort to remember a particularly peaceful time that I could recall emotionally. Days, weeks passed without success. It began to look as if Anthony Newley's advice would have to be tried. In many ways it frightened me the most: to trust enough to do nothing.

On the day. It was the final day of the location shooting. I had to come up with something. As I was guided to my mark on the floating galleon I remember thinking: Well, Newley, here we go! The sun was out and Krasker's lighting was a bit less harsh than usual, or maybe my eyes were building up resistance to it. I stood on my mark, closed my eyes and faced into the hottest area of the light. I could feel the sun on my face, a gentle sea breeze, the noose swinging in it and occasionally touching my face. Here we go, I thought. Then paused my thoughts and waited.

'Stand by!'

A little song came into my head. I tried for a moment to get back to an empty head. And then in a flash …

'Turn over.'

An old moment came back to me. I am sitting on the floor in front of Granny Kate's coal-burning fire stove doing my homework. My gran is in the scullery fixing me a marmalade sandwich. She is singing softly to herself 'Little Dolly Daydream'. As I heard the refrain, my being began vibrating to another music. I was experiencing a previously unknown joy. Somehow not mine yet within me.

'Action!'

Listening to it as the noose slipped over my head, I slowly faced the mutinous crew.

'Cut!'

Ustinov smiles to me. He turns to Robert Krasker, who nods. Ustinov looks toward the sound team. OK.

He smiles again to me.

'I feel we got that, folks.'

It was to be the final shot in the film for me.

I shall go deeper into what happened to me during that take as it was my very first step into a new standpoint that would change the direction of my life.

As the song vibrated through me, I became aware of a subtle shift in my feelings and a warm emotional sensation permeated through me. It wasn't like anything I had ever felt before and too fragile to even put a name to. It vibrated through me. There was never a question of whether it was appropriate. It just was. Instinctively I knew. Curiously I never spoke of it with anyone; it was too personal, too private. Sometimes when I pondered on it I realised it was in me but not of me, in the sense that I could not summon it, it was outside my control. It somehow represented the best in me yet I looked on it as an otherness, and as from time to time it was there (always between 'Action' and 'Cut') it was never the same, I began to appreciate it as the ever-strange otherness.

A side effect of this phenomenon was I became conscious of the fact that in performance a thought can be better conveyed to another than a word. And a feeling put into words becomes half-dead. It was later when *Billy Budd* was screened with an audience that I understood that feeling, in its own sphere, is fully living, and not only reaches the feelings of others and can be transported by the movie camera.

However, while I was in limbo waiting for the release of Ustinov's film, my agent James Fraser received

Shock therapy from Laurence Olivier

a telephone call from Laurence Olivier, who was putting together a cast of players to launch a new theatre in Chichester. Would I be interested?

Of course I was interested: what parts did he have in mind for me? When Jimmy enquired, Olivier replied 'Oh, forget it' and hung up. An untested burgeoning ego was the last thing he was looking for apparently.

For the *Billy Budd* role I received £900, and of course I began thinking of made-to-measure shoes, when the possibility of a second film came up. It was a small part, two weeks' work spread over ten weeks. It was entitled *Term of Trial*, to be directed by Peter Glenville, starring Laurence Olivier, Simone Signoret, and showcasing an unknown girl in her debut film, one Sarah Miles.

I got along fine with Sarah, yet I could see she was a bit of a handful.

She only had eyes for Olivier. This was not a memorable shoot for me, albeit in Ireland. Thinking back over the time I experience a benign forgetfulness, save for a run-in with Olivier. In our first scene together, he's a teacher, I am an errant pupil, his opening salvo to me was:

'It's good you didn't join the Chichester troupe, your voice wouldn't be up to it.'

He obviously wasn't concerned with his own delivery, as it sounded clipped and rather high-pitched. I retorted: 'My voice? What about your voice, you think you sound great?'

Billy, by permission of Robert Krascer. He made me look better on film than I did in real life.

He was speechless for a moment, no doubt taken aback by what he regarded as an East End spiv giving as good as he got.

'Oh, well, it's only since *The Entertainer*', he replied, naming his last role.

Fortunately, the director was ready to shoot and our exchange was designated to the cutting room.

Alone in my hotel that evening, memorising my lines for the next scene, I thought how had I begun on such a wrong note. This was the best Henry V I'd ever seen, to say nothing of his Richard III. Our next encounter couldn't have been more different. On the set together, his head close to mine, in his dulcet Prince of Denmark voice: 'You should always work on your voice, Terence, as when your looks fade the voice continues to be empowered.' Encouraged by his warmth, I asked: 'Did you ever meet John Barrymore?' 'Caught his Hamlet at the Haymarket when I was a teenager, mesmerising. Now there was an actor with a voice. Well, he had everything.'

I honestly have no idea what prompted his turnaround, perhaps he saw something of his own youthful rebellion in me. Maybe he'd discussed it with his wife, the amazing Joan Plowright. The bottom line was he inspired me, suffice to say I have worked on my voice and breath ever since.

Looking back over life, it is apparent to what lengths I went to prove my worth to my Mum and Dad. The premiere of *Billy Budd* is a perfect example of this. I hadn't seen any rushes or clips of the work. Yet I went to great lengths to get Tom and Ethel to this Leicester Square premiere.

I always conveyed the practicalities of the big evening to my Mother, who could barely control her excitement. My Dad's reserved presence appeared unruffled. They would organise a local car to get them to the Leicester Square Cinema for 7.30, the get home would be down to me. The film company would be providing transport for Samantha Eggar, my date, and myself.

Evidently at about 6pm my Dad wasn't getting into his threads and announced to Ethel he wasn't going.

Not to be deterred, Mum ducked out to the public phone box in Prince Regent Lane and rang her sister Julie.

'Don't pay any notice to him. Those Stamps are a funny lot. I'll ring you a car from the guy up the road. It'll be there in minutes. You go on your own.'

At the last moment my Dad had a change of heart and presented himself dressed with a clean shirt and a nice tie.

When I finally heard about the incident, it gave me an insight into my Dad's seemingly emotional armour.

Even today it's difficult to imagine how the night could have been improved. You can see in the photos what it meant to Tom and Ethel, yet for my part two things occurred which reverberate to this day.

Such a shock it was to see myself up there on the big screen, looking as I had never looked in life, courtesy of Peter Ustinov and the diminutive giant of the light, Robert Krasker. On reflection, my decision to concentrate my energies solely on celluloid was made that night, and whilst I didn't see life in such terms then, I must have realised the universe was telling me something. The second implosion was my final scene in the film, ending with Herman Melville's line, 'God bless Captain Vere'.

The transcendental moment that had happened to me on that single last take on location left not a dry eye in the house. And while it was the last thing I was aware of that evening, my sails became set for new horizons.

After the premiere the Ustinovs took the Stamps, Samantha and me to the White Elephant, in one of my favourite streets in London, Curzon

Street. Peter discovered my Dad liked a drop of cognac, and my Dad discovered his wisecracks cracked up the great man. A good deal of the restaurant's best 1906 was downed, and Sam and I dropped off Tom and Ethel back to 124 Chadwin at around 3.30am.

Years later I asked my Mum: 'What precisely happened after we dropped you home?'

'I asked your Dad what he wanted to do and he said, "You put the kettle on and make us a pot of tea, then you can get your head down and I'll get on my bike and catch the tide at the Isle of Dogs".'

Many years later, I was stopped in the street by a tall imposing guy about my own age who asked, 'Are you Tom Stamp's boy?'

'I am', I said. 'What made you ask?'

'You walk just like yer Dad', he replied.

'You knew my Dad then?'

'I worked with him at the Union Lighterage. I was his lad on the Bronco [my Dad's tug].'

When I came to know Robert Lockwood better, he owned an art supply shop off Regent Street and supplied me with left-handed calligraphic pens, I asked him if he was working that day after the *Billy Budd* premiere.

'Oh sure', he said.

'You do?'

'Cannot forget, none of us knew anything about you being in a movie but that afternoon when the Bronco docked back at the Isle of Dogs one of the other crew was holding up an *Evening News* with a photo of you and your Mum and Dad on the front page. "What's all this, then, Tom?" he asked. Your Dad had a good look at the paper and after a minute he said, "Ee's a very lucky boy".'

5

We're not making the book. We're going to make a love story, modern.

William Wyler

Billy Budd was extremely well received by critics and the public, so well in fact that it left my agent Jimmy Fraser and myself with a conundrum: Should we wait for another good film to present itself or should we grab the cash that other producers were offering hoping to cash in the success of Ustinov's masterwork?

During the time Mike Caine and I had shared digs, he had often lectured me on this point. Basically it was always better to do the good work, was his unequivocal advice. As he was older and the first working actor I felt I could take advice from, I did. That early philosophy was to direct my steps in the industry.

The fee I received from *Term of Trial* was more than enough to pay the rent, and finally John Fowles' first book *The Collector* came within my wavelength. I went to see John Kohn and Judd Kinberg and left the interview with the galleys of the book, which I started to read on the bus home. Gosh, it was a splendidly written piece, yet as soon as I was drawn into it the

illian Wyler and Samantha

realisation came that I would be completely wrong for the part: an invisible, spotty, runny-nosed bank clerk. I passed. Jimmy Fraser went along with me. He may have had his own opinions as the project had been picked up by Columbia Pictures. Both producers kept in touch with Fraser and Dunlop, and Jimmy kept me abreast of their interest, but I just couldn't see myself as the character.

This was cinema, not the stage. A good make-up job wouldn't cut it. Weeks went by then the call came. William Wyler had agreed to direct the film. Was I going to turn down Wyler, arguably the most critically and commercially successful director in the business and who Laurence Olivier credited with fundamentally changing how he viewed motion pictures?

'Does Wyler want me?'

'It looks that way', Jimmy Fraser replied.

'Are you sure?'

'It appears so. What's your worry?'

'I can't see a way to do it. Who's the girl?'

'They are going to test some actresses. The director Bob Parrish is shooting the tests. Mr Wyler is going to fly over to see them.'

I suddenly had an idea.

'Why don't I do the tests with the girls? At least Wyler will be able to see how close I can get to the part.'

'Good thought. I'll call John and Judd.'

I consequently tested with Sarah Miles and Samantha Eggar. Bob Parrish was terrifically supportive.

A few days later I was summoned to the old Columbia headquarters in Wardour Street. I was shown to a vestibule on the second floor at one end of a long corridor. Doors opened and closed, quickly. Then a door at the far end of the passage opened and a diminutive man came out. All the other doors closed. The man walked mindfully in my direction. As he moved closer I became aware of his eyes taking me in. His look was calm, steady yet unrelenting. I became self-conscious and looked down. He stopped directly in front of me, quite close. 'I've seen the tests', were the first words I'd hear from the voice that had directed Montgomery Clift, the voice that had taught Laurence Olivier the finer points of performing for the camera.

'Which girl d'you like?' I stammered.

Looking directly into my eyes he said, 'I haven't looked at them yet.'

As the implication of this statement reached me, I said, 'D'you want me?'

His glance didn't waver. He nodded. Yes.

'But in the book ... ' I began.

He cut me short, and placing his arm around my shoulders drew me close to him. He smelled spicy. 'I'm not going to make the book', he whispered. 'Going to make a love story, modern. And you're going to be purrfect.'

And so it began. My very first Hollywood adventure.

On noticing how friendly Sam and I were, Wyler advised me to distance myself. 'This will help her as she grows to dislike your character and it will enable you to feel possession for her. Many men possess women whilst believing they love them. It's fine if they want to be possessed, but Miranda doesn't, she is smarter than Freddie, yet it doesn't help her escape. Your presence is powered by your possessiveness. The more present you are the more frightening you will be.'

Robert Surtees was Willie's choice of lighting cameraman, and as the film was to be in colour I expected my difficulties with the intensity of light to be worse than in black-and-white. Yet Surtees made it easier. Firstly, the Los Angeles portion of the shoot was all interiors, the exteriors would follow in the UK. This would seem to make the shoot more expensive and a required complete change of crew for both continents, yet Mike Frankovich had just been appointed the chief of Columbia Pictures and Wyler told me Mike wanted to be seen as bringing productions to Hollywood. I didn't give much thought to this scheduling as I was as happy as a sandboy to be alongside Wyler and opposite an actress as ravishing as Samantha.

Whilst Wyler was as brilliant as his reputation foretold, he was a joy of a guy to be with. One day I came back from lunch to see Willie conversing with a woman of a similar age, a little distance from the set. I observed from a polite distance. Eventually his visitor left and he made his way to me. I started in on him immediately.

'Seeing chicks on the set, eh, Willie? Who was that, does your wife know you are having these assignations while you're supposed to be at work?'

Wyler just went along with it. He was listening to me yet I could see he had something on his mind. When I ran out of steam he said in a considered tone:

'Do you remember all the women you've slept with?'

'Of course. Don't you?'

'No. And I feel I should. It affects how I say "Hello".'

It was a really nice surprise when the shoot relocated to England – Kent, as it happened – and I discovered Bob Krasker, the DP who had done so well by me as Billy Budd, was lighting the exteriors, this time in colour.

I couldn't overlook how well my work was working out, the opportunity I had learning from a great man like Wyler so early in my career, and how the fundamentals he made clear to me would equip me later when I encountered lesser directors, and even one who didn't want me at all.

There was no repetition of the brief moment of elation I felt at the conclusion of *Billy Budd*, yet with Wyler's support and seeming satisfaction with the performance I began to become more familiar with what I felt was being present prior to 'Action': Present and being conscious of being present is how I related to it.

Whilst awaiting the release of *The Collector*, Joe Janni, a creative producer of the highest order, approached me about featuring with the Italian actress Monica Vitti in a film of the popular cartoon, *Modesty Blaise*. She was Michelangelo Antonioni's star and lover, who resembled the drawn character of Modesty. The piece was to be directed by Joseph Losey. By the time the shoot began, Dirk Bogarde had been cast to play the bad guy. His sucking up to Losey was hard to watch during the shoot, as I had previously admired Losey's work. Yet it paid off for Dirk: his camp, naff villain became the lead in the finished movie, with Modesty and Willie Garvin, my part, reduced to ineffectual sketches. I'd heard tales of Dirk's narcissism which I didn't believe until my experience of observing him.

The Collector was a Wyler classic;, Samantha and I won the Best Actress and Best Actor awards respectively at Cannes 1965, and she was nominated for an Academy Award.

6

'L'obsede?' she enquired.

The predilection for big hotels started as soon as I began making films and has continued ever since. Whenever I awoke on that first morning in a hotel I hadn't stayed in before, the possibilities of the coming day were enhanced.

It happened in the Lancaster in Paris, and on this occasion my intimations were not exaggerated. Suzanne Cloutier, Mrs Ustinov, who in no small part had been responsible for Peter casting me as *Billy Budd*, had told me that the French would appreciate my work. She had been Orson Welles' Desdemona in his *Othello*, yet as importantly, in my case, she had known the French actor Gerard Philippe. In one of our early chats, she and me, she'd told me she had informed her husband that I possessed a lot of Gerard's qualities when on film. Later she'd made sure I did French media and even recommended I equip myself with a Louis Vuitton suitcase.

'You can only buy them in France and not many English or Americans know of them.'

Consequently, when Samantha Eggar and I both won the Cannes Festival Acting Award, I attended the Paris premiere, which is how I came to be waking up in the Lancaster Hotel. I did most of the interviews in the suite, and after a bite I wandered the public rooms, familiarising myself with the sumptuous quarters.

Almost immediately I espied a young lady leaning indecently against a high-backed chair in the ground floor lounge. Her posture struck me as larger-than-life and as I came further into the room I fully expected a fashion photographer and crew to be featuring her. Yet the room was empty save for us. As she seemed unaware of my presence I was able to observe her at leisure. She proved to be unusually beautiful, a blonde with devastatingly curly hair, a perfect pair of legs, most of which were visible as she was wearing the very latest of short frocks. I was moving in for a close-up when she changed the direction of her look: seeing me, she smiled. The effects of this smile were twofold. As my attention was so completely on her, you could say I was absent, so it took me a moment to realise the smile was for me, and when I returned, my response, even if I had only been an eye-line for her close shot, was gormless. The second was the smile itself. The mouth, which had been commanding my attention, was itself almost unreal; the lips were as deep as they were wide, so the overall image was almost a perfect sphere, and when it moved the unreality of its shape assumed a normality.

I managed a grin and suddenly felt conscious as her attention on me matched my own blatant stare.

'*L'obsede?*' she enquired. *The Collector* in French. Her voice was gentle, unforced.

'I'm afraid so', I replied.

'I should be afraid', she said in English.

'I wouldn't go that far.' That raised a smile. 'And you are?'

She opened her lips to make an O.

'O', I said. 'Your name is O?'

There followed a silence, not uncomfortable.

'Can I buy you a coffee?'

She looked about her.

'Are you expecting someone?'

'Not exactly.'

'We could go to my suite, it's more private.'

'Would you imprison me?'

'I might. If you don't do what I want.'

The lips protruded forward: 'Ooo!'

I moved towards the stairs, fully expecting to exit alone, yet she followed.

As I put my key in the door, she took in the number.

'55', she commented. 'A very good number. Double fun.'

'Do you study numbers?'

'I study lots of things.'

I bet, I thought.

Once inside the main room, she requested the bathroom, yet re-emerged almost without pause. I wondered what had occurred. She sat on the floor, pulled her knees up and spread her legs like a ballet dancer.

There was no leotard or panties in evidence. Only another perfect O of lips, bordered by another circle of neat curly blonde hair. I dropped my strides and knelt in front of her. She drew her fingers across her vagina, they crossed near my face as I lowered my face into her. I caught an aroma of patchouli. She was more than ready. I eased my rod into her to the hilt, my own black public hair pressing right against her hot blonde ones.

About to begin motion, I felt her hands on my buttocks.

She said, 'I do it.'

I then became aware of what I can only describe as the inner walls of her vagina wafting around the head of my erection. Every time I made a move to compliment this she pressed her fingers into me and whispered close to my ear, 'Ssh, be still'.

This went on for some time and as we both began to show signs of nearing climax she altered the position of her hand and placed her fingers firmly on my urethra under the pudental area that joined my anus and the underside of my testicles.

'Release', she commanded. 'Using your breath visualise the ejaculation being drawn up your spine.'

Feeling completely at her mercy, I did as instructed.

After the unique event where organism was actually separate from ejaculation, I relaxed with wonder. Some time passed; she gently slid off me and inspected the tip for leakage. 'Bien,' she commented. 'Safe.' I was considering the ramifications of this reabsorption of ether (sperm). With another of her knowing smiles: 'Less recovery time now needed,' as she suggestively slipped onto her tummy. My first collaborator in the art of tantric sex evidently had different ramifications in mind.

The next time I met Suzanne Cloutier she had studied how the French press received Wyler's film and asked me about my experiences in Paris. Of course she soon wheedled out of me my unforgettable meeting in Rue de Berri.

'So you haven't seen her again?'

'No, she was quite firm about that.'

'Hmm.'

'She was so unusual. Beautiful, yet a one-off. I felt sure she would be in show business in some way.'

'No.' She paused for some time and then: 'Now don't take this the wrong way, because what I'm telling you is almost unique to France.'

Another pause. 'There is a unique class of women here. A unique class of courtesans, which is known yet rarely discussed, originally for royalty, aristocrats, but now a selected trade for huge fees.'

'She never asked me for a cent—', I protested.

'Well, it's a great compliment for you. If I'm right, she obviously just fancied you, she may even have been waiting for you at the hotel. She'd apparently seen your film.'

That caused me to pause. She had indeed called the shots.

'Did you get a Vuitton?'

I laughed. As we were saying goodbye, I asked her for directions to the shop, and she said:

'The ones they are selling now are elegant enough but ask them if they have a case from the Fifties, I think they are a better style.'

I often think of her when packing the old suitcase I purchased that day. The day of my first experience of Tantric Sex.

7

'I read the news today oh boy'

'A Day in the Life', Lennon-McCartney, 1967

I am frequently asked about London in the Sixties, for me the most memorable was the new working-class rock'n'roll raj. And their availability. Running into John Lennon outside the Casserole, we strolled and chatted the length of the Kings Road. What an interesting guy. To hear that music in his ears for the very first time and then put lyrics to it.

What must it have been like for Lennon and McCartney to awake one morning and hear a life-changing melody before anyone else alive.

Joe Janni didn't blame yours truly for the disaster that *Modesty Blaise* became, as he approached me for his next film, Thomas Hardy's *Far from the Madding Crowd*. John Schlesinger would direct. The classic would star Julie Christie, Alan Bates and Peter Finch. Of course I jumped at the chance, even though it later became clear that Schlesinger actually wanted somebody else. Evidently he

Bathsheba and Seargent Troy

preferred blonds himself and wanted Jon Voight. Fortunately for me, Janni insisted I should play Sergeant Troy. So off I went to live in Dorset for three months. What a ravishing location it was too.

It is 1966. London is in full swing. An extraordinary man named Geoffrey Bennison, known to his night time pals as Big Carol, has taken me to visit his friend John Richardson, the Picasso authority, who lives in The Albany, Piccadilly. I had been introduced to Geoffrey when I rented an apartment in Mount Street and he'd helped me decorate and furnish it. When I'd moved in and he came for a cuppa, I recall him saying, 'This is OK for now, dear, but isn't there anywhere you'd like to live long term?' As a youth employed as a messenger boy in Cheapside, I had delivered a package to the quiet chambers in St James and had never forgotten them.

'I couldn't get a place there but I'd love to just see inside one', I'd replied. Which is how I wound up having coffee with Geoffrey and Mr Richardson in his august set in Albany. When he was showing us out onto the charms of the Henry Holland rope walk, I found the courage to say, 'If you ever hear of anything possibly for rent, would you let Geoffrey know. I'd love to be a resident here.'

Carol Edge and me in the Kyoto I constructed in Piccadilly

Now when the Universe opens, it really opens. Within a month D1 came up for rent and I was moving the Barcelona chairs purchased for 119 Mount Street into my very own Georgian chambers in St James.

Bennison also introduced me to another of his chums, the artist Francis Bacon. I got to know him better with Lionel Bart, as he and Bacon were neighbours in Reece Mews off South Kensington Underground.

One time Lionel popped in to see Francis and followed him into his kitchen, where he was making them something to drink. Lionel was taken aback by the many photographs displayed on Francis's kitchen wall, and saw one of yours truly.

'What's Stamp doing on your wall, Francis?' he asked.

'Oh', replied Francis, 'the two best looking guys around are Terence Stamp and Colonel Gaddafi.'

While I was in Mount Street I was introduced to Douglas Hayward. Doug was a tailor who had apprenticed himself to a master named Dimmie

Major, working out of Fulham. Doug felt he was ready to branch out on his own and asked me to look out for a property for a shop in the West End. I noticed a vacant clothes cleaning shop up the road from me. It still had its 'By Appointment' transfer on the window. I said to Doug, 'You should check it out; if it's right for you, leave the seal on the front window.' Doug snapped it up and it became one of the focal points in Mayfair when the new tailor's establishment opened its doors, in no small part due to Doug's amazing welcoming and humorous personality, to say nothing of the cut and line of the whistles he and Major outfitted all the dressers in showbiz with.

Six weeks before the start of the *Madding Crowd* shoot the director informed my agent that prior to 1860 no left-handed solders were allowed in the cavalry division of Hardy's epic, and I would have to master the sabre with my right hand or be replaced. Joe Janni arranged for a master of the sabre to come to my new chambers to teach me. I came into the world favouring my left hand, and it was the first time I'd had occasion to feature my right hand in anything so special.

Feeling a bit downcast after the initial instruction and the enormity of the task Schlesinger had set for me, I dropped into Doug's new shop, the front space of which had become the new chic male club in town.

Chris and I with my first Roller, outside the Albany

'I've got just the job to cheer you up', Doug said. And without any further comment, we strolled to a dingy, minute basement in Cork Street. That afternoon I met a master craftsman of footwear, George Cleverley. He'd fashioned the boots for Rudolph Valentino in *Blood and Sand*, yet more importantly for yours truly he shod my idol Gary Cooper. The first shoes he made for me were a pair of Monks, fumed oak calf stained down, £25. Still worn today! Albeit, enriched by the passage of time.

Joe Janni and John Schlesinger had starred Julie in *Billy Liar* and *Darling*, and Alan Bates had made *A Kind of Loving* for Schlesinger, so they both were happy working with him, but Peter Finch hadn't a good word to say about him, often berating him loudly in front of the crew.

My own excursions to Jalal ud-din Rumi's birthplace in Persia were still in the future, so I hadn't come across 'the smiling forehead' philosophy of viewing whatever life brought your way with acceptance. Although it soon occurred to me I couldn't let a great role go to waste because the director liked his boys blond. Salvation came in the shape of Nicolas Roeg.

Nic was being acknowledged as a new gift to the world of film lighting, and Joe Janni had spotted him and tipped off his director. He and I really hit it off and when he saw how little shooting time was being given to Sergeant Troy's sword exercise, the sequence in which Troy initially woos Bathsheba (Julie). He suggested we do extra set-ups when the official work for the day finished. Whenever there was a spectacular sunset he would wink at me and say, 'Get your sword'.

I would don my red uniform, grab the sabre, he would likewise grab one of the hand-held film cameras, and we would set off to where the original, albeit sparse, sequence had been shot. Probably why Finch referred to John as a TV director.

On arriving in Weymouth I had borrowed the property master's back-up sabre and continued my practices daily before and after work, becoming proficient with both hands. When Nic realised this, he had me doing all manner of things with the sword, wielding it from hand to hand, etc. It was chiefly down to Nic that the sword sequence in the film was so sexy, and folks I meet today still recall it as one of the most memorable scenes in the film. Nicolas Roeg had a very distinguished career as a director after *Madding Crowd*, which didn't surprise me. Although I was sorry he never asked me to work with him when he was officially at the helm.

It was a privilege to work with Julie. So good, so beautiful. Strangely, she always doubted this herself, and I guess it was this modesty that ennobled the inner radiance that the camera fell so in love with. Working with her was a trip, as I watched her become the still, quiet performer when she stepped up to her mark, and her very being was presented for the camera. People often talk to me about the magnetism of Julie's eyes, yet take it from me it's the timeless presence that streams liquid light into those sapphire minces. The 'eye of the beholder' indeed for JC.

Towards the end of the shoot, Joe Janni approached me about his next film. He'd come upon a new director, Ken Loach, who had just completed his first feature for TV, and Joe was intending to make his second on film, which would star the actress Carol White, so touching as Cathy in Loach's *Cathy Come Home*.

Joe wanted a bankable actor to play a supporting role. His problem was he didn't have a proper budget and needed me to work for free... naturally with a generous back-end, which usually meant the same as the up-front salary, i.e. nothing.

The other drawback was that he didn't have a screenplay, as Loach was intending to improvise all the dialogue. Joe told me the outline. My role would only take a couple of weeks, all in London. As Joe had been so supportive of me during the *Modesty Blaise*/Dirk Bogarde fiasco, even insisting Schlesinger hire me after it, I felt well-disposed to him. Also, whilst I didn't voice it, the idea of throwing myself into the void without scripted dialogue in front of the camera was scary but exciting. At the end of our chat, Joe asked me: 'Terence, are you political?'

'Not in the least', I replied.

Joe grinned.

'So you're not concerned with getting a title?'

'Terence is more than enough title for me. I need for nothing.'

'Terence Stamp would be more than enough for most men!'

'Why d'you ask?'

'Oh yes. Ken is a left-winger. He fights for the underprivileged.'

'He can fight for who he likes, as long as he's a good director.'

'He's that alright.'

Which is how I wound up featuring in *Poor Cow*. Ken was delightful to work with and it was a big plus working alongside Miss White as she was used to Ken's methodology. The lighting Ken didn't use much, the set-ups were pacey filmmaking for me, yet the actual shooting was different as we hadn't any dialogue. Just prior to the take Ken would give both of us a rough outline of the subjects he needed for his trajectory, and off we would go. We rarely did more than one take. It was as comfortable a fit for yours truly as the white buckskin brogues that George Cleverley fashioned for me after searching for years for pelts that were 'just right'.

I had met a diminutive New Yorker courtesy of my brother Chris, who was managing The Who and had spotted Jimi Hendrix: he and Kit Lambert, his partner, secured him for their new label Track Records. The Yank was named Pete Kameron, and was bringing Chris up to speed on the music business. He offered to negotiate my back-end deal for *Poor Cow*. I didn't know at the time that it was practically unheard of to get any cash out of film companies after the shoot, which is the reason artists demand it up front.

I hadn't come across many black people growing up, save for one boy in another year at Tolgate Primary. So it was a memorable occasion when my brother Chris introduced me to Jimi Hendrix shortly after I witnessed his concert at the Savile Theatre, and he became the first black guy I had a close association with.

There are two archetypes of princes: the first by bloodline and the second by nature. The first don't always conduct themselves as aristocrats, as their outlook is learned, studied, and vested interests are at stake. To the latter, their behaviour comes naturally as they know nothing else. Jimi was one of those - a prince. 'I read the news today, oh boy.'

Jimi Hendrix passed away on the 18th September, 1970.

One of the things that sticks in my mind about my Dad is that he had a veritable knack of finding money in the street. No denomination passed unnoticed, be it large or small. He pocketed all, from pennies to silver, even to carefully folded notes. He wasn't a gambling man. In fact I only recall him studiously filling in his Sherman's Football Pool every week in the hope of winning the £75,000 prize, a fortune at the time. Which is probably why, when Chris hit it big with Hendrix and The Who, our Dad woke up one morning after a riotously boozy night with Chris and our youngest brother John to discover the cheque for 75 big ones that Chris had left in the pocket of Tom's sheepskin coat. Even this event didn't quell his cash-on-the-pavement ability.

He apparently bequeathed his gift to me when he changed his cosmic address. I guess I began to lower my glance as I often became aware of money on the sidewalk. I stooped for all, always acknowledging my Dad with a 'Thanks, Tom'.

This continued until I began studying the Bates Eye Method with the aptly named Miss Sage, who explained to me that the eye is designed to view everything evenly on its curved circumference. If the side vision isn't used regularly, i.e. predominantly featuring front focus, the intelligence of the mind says to itself, 'He isn't using his side vision, we'll shut that down and use the energy elsewhere.' I reinstituted my peripheral vision by defocusing on the straight ahead or down, looking and observing what I am passing on both sides.

'Watch what's leaving!' Evelyn Sage advised.

It has curtailed my picking-up-cash abilities. I don't find dropped coins in the Burlington Arcade any more, as its Georgian paralleled shops are a perfect reminder for me to switch to using my peripheral vision.

Poor Cow was a much magnified example of the unexpected cash find, as the film received ecstatic reviews and within months I'd made more money than I'd ever earned before. Unfortunately those were the days when all monies above £20,000 annually were super-taxed. In other words, the recipient gets sixpence and the Revenue gets the nineteen shillings and sixpence. *Poor Cow* indeed.

I had been lucky to be discovered by a great agent, who I stayed with for thirty years. James Fraser became one of my best pals. You could even say I loved him. The times when the phone didn't ring I assumed he was still looking for jobs for me. If you don't believe your agent holds the best for you at all times, find another. Most work-related memorable times began with Jimmy's Scottish burr. Orson was no different.

In 1967, James Fraser, the first and only professional to witness my Iago, asked me if I would like to go to Paris to meet Orson Welles. Is a maraschino cherry red?

The following evening, I arrive at the designated restaurant. As I enter the cavernous space, all painted white, my eye is drawn to the only occupant. He is sitting against the far wall, dressed in black. It is, of course, Mr Welles. I track in to get a close up, breathing deeply to fill the space between us.

We shake hands. He indicates the chair opposite him and I sit down.

'Are you travelling alone?' I ask.

The reply rumbles toward me from under the table and over it.

'It depends.'

I glance around at the table set for a lot more than two and ask, 'Are a lot of people joining us?'

'It's you and me for now. But I tend to accumulate,' he says with the famous grin. 'You OK with red?'

A waiter has arrived with a bottle, extracts the cork and gives Orson a taste. After he pours us both a glass, he places the bottle beside me. Throughout the evening, while I was never aware of my host taking a drink, he regularly leaned over and nudged me to refill his glass, which had magically emptied itself.

He had a script from a Spanish classic called *Divine Words* which he wanted me to read. He would get it to me. I had the impression he approved of my showing up alone. It was noticeable throughout the evening that whenever I revealed a new facet of myself, he seamlessly accommodated me and broadened his responses. Years later I experienced the same attitude in President Bill Clinton.

After highlighting a few of the specialities on the menu, all meat dishes, I was forced to confess I was a vegetarian. He didn't pause, and with the same enthusiasm reeled off a few without meat. Charm is a maligned word these days, yet Orson Welles bore witness to its original meaning. It was as natural to him as whistling is to the wind.

As the evening progressed and I became more comfortable in his presence, I asked him why he had such a hard time putting films together, considering the depth of his genius and the dross that was increasingly being produced.

'The trouble began with Kane', he answered. 'Or rather its inspiration, William Randolph Hearst – the big man with the thin but far reaching voice.'

I knew what he meant. It was said that the publishing magnate's influence was so great that by use of media which he'd controlled, he had pushed the United States into war with Spain at the turn of the century. Destroying the career of a film director would have been no problem for Hearst.

According to a story I'd recently heard, Ronan O'Rahilly, the founder of Radio Caroline, had commissioned a script for Orson, with the money in place to make the film. The night before the cheque was to be signed, O'Rahilly was at a dinner party with the backer. Some friends of the publishing magnate were also at the table and conversation turned to the upcoming movie and its director. Things were said and warnings issued. By morning the backer and his backing had vanished. I know about this because one of the parts had been written with me in mind.

'Is that why you're planning to shoot this one in Spain?' I asked.

'It is where the money is. I can shoot anywhere.' Again the famous smile. And then: 'I'm a high wire act. I guess you are, too.'

'I'd tell you if I knew what you meant.'

'No safety net. Oven fresh, when you perform.'

'When I'm out there, I aspire to it. Haven't cracked it on the stage though.'

'You'll get there.'

Encouraged by the turn of the conversation, I asked: 'Any tips?'

After tapping my arm and indicating his empty glass, he considered. 'The moment before you go on ... assure yourself you're going to get to the end. That's what opera singers do. The more you trust in the muse, the more she'll be there for you.'

'Can you tell me how you feel the muse?'

He smiled. 'No.' Another smile. 'If we do the movie, we'll have lots to talk about.'

I held his glance. Would I ever get another chance? 'I bet you can describe her ... Queen Mab.'

He looked at me anew. Truly engaging me. There was a pause until, finally, he said, 'It's one manifesting through the many.'

His answer was in keeping with Shakespeare's intention of Queen Mab, the fairy midwife from *Romeo and Juliet*, helping sleepers give birth to their dreams.

But then, why wouldn't his answer be spot-on? Orson knew all about dreams, about their inspiration and struggle towards fulfilment.

I wanted more, but by then the room had begun to full up and, hearing his famous voice, other diners came over to shake his hand. Some accepting his openness, sat down; an impromptu audience, at which I was a courtier. Orson had energy and time for everyone.

After Orson died, Jeanne Moreau said of him: 'He was a king without a country.' To me, he was royalty whose domain was his own aura. The wonderful treatment of *Divine Words* didn't happen. He failed to raise the bread.

'Smiling forehead': It's in the eye of the beholder! What is in the eye of the beholder, presuming who or what is looking? Which was part of a mystery I learned about when I was studying to whirl like a dervish. The 'smiling forehead' is imbued with your view of the world, and the people and events life presents you with. If a 'bad' one viewed as possibly good – I believe Wagner was ridiculed when he was originally listened to, and a 'good' possibly bad: there is an innate relaxation in the mind which affects the forehead which smiles inwardly. Of course it goes without saying a certain awareness of the labelling tendency of thought, as it happens, is crucial.

8

Blue. And the fastest gun in the West.

Now it's worth a mention that my beloved mother's favourite film of mine was *Far From the Madding Crowd*, so it couldn't have been all bad. Yet I suspect she approved of the way her eldest son looked wielding the Victorian sabre in his bright red tunic. Conversely, a young lady I now think of as the future ex-wife claims the best appearance for her was in

Blue, the western I made for Silvio Narizzano soon after my foray in Dorset.

The director was a wonderfully upbeat fella, as his moniker suggests. One of his earlier films was entitled *Georgy Girl* and I'd loved it. So I was happy to go along with his vision of my character as a blond and submit myself to the peroxide bottle again. I was more experienced those days and more conscious of what the hair department was doing to my head a couple of hours every fortnight. I came to understand what the girls went through and of course realised that the hair on my head grew at the same rate as the hair on my chin.

I never thought I'd be the fastest gun in the west, or use both hands

Yet it was the second discipline that I subjected myself to that shined a different light on my earlier arduous sabre exercises. The cowboy I was attempting to portray wore two pistols and could shoot well and, more importantly, fast-draw. I was assigned a gentleman known in the business as the 'fastest gun in the West'. Bolstered by the man himself and the fact that my right hand had been roused successfully from its lifelong slumber, I used my natural tendency for being a good pupil to stand me in good stead. What emerged – which was to have long-lasting ramifications – was that my teacher made clear to me, after considerable tuition and practice, that my right hand was faster than my left. I was incredulous, disbelieving, yet the master was unwavering. By way of explanation he put forward the theory that in this split-second skill, originally involving life and death, the over-used left hand was encumbered with hundreds of memorised actions, whilst the other hand was not. He pointed out that left-handed gunmen had a differing outlook to their right-handed compatriots, in that the left hand was primarily prompted by the right hemisphere of the brain, which involved the wholeness or big picture of life, while the left hemisphere was more concerned with the details. At our last session together he suggested that in the future I should try to become more ambidextrous, thereby balancing the two hemispheres.

'Before you start loading your sidearms with live ammo, brush your teeth with both hands, shave with both hands. Embrace new skills with your right hand.'

Coincidentally, as I scribble, tomorrow is the spring equinox: it is one of two days every year when night and day are equal, a unique moment of cosmic balance.

Consequently, these days I use chopsticks in my right hand and can even use a cutthroat razor to shave both sides of my face.

From the standpoint of the smiling forehead, John Schlesinger was doing me a long-term good turn when he dragged me into the arena of ambidextrousness.

One of the best things about making films is the locations you go to, always hand-picked. My shoots in the US never failed to impress me. Moab, Utah for *Blue* was one of them, and being lit by Stanley Cortez made it extra special. Co-star Joanna Pettet was another. The allure and charm of our locations during *Blue* have stayed with me. And I have always been drawn to the spaces of the US where the earth is red.

9

'I don't want to play the part. I'm a bastard.'

Peter O'Toole

When I returned to London having completed the western, I was still waiting for my unbleached hair to grow back in when I was summoned to my agent Jimmy Fraser's offices in Regent Street.

'I've just had a call from a casting agent round the corner. He's been contacted by Fellini in Rome. "Send me your most decadent actors!" was his brief. He immediately rang to discuss your availability.'

'Is that how I am thought of in the business?'

'Don't concern yourself with that.'

'Who else is going?'

'I don't know.'

'When does the shoot start?'

'In a fortnight!'

'A fortnight?'

He nodded, yes.

'Sounds like somebody's dropped out.'

'Somebody has.'

'Come on, don't be coy. It doesn't suit you.'

Jimmy grinned. O'Toole.

'Peter O'Toole. O'Toole had been pestering Fellini to work with him, so when the project came on line, Fellini wrote it with him in mind. Apparently O'Toole was delighted, but when he was sent the script he changed his mind. Do you still want to go?'

'Listen, Jim, I probably won't get the job if he's conceived it with O'Toole in mind. Yet if I only get to meet Fellini it's worth the trip.'

I was recalling some of my favourite films the great director had made. *Nights of Cabiria*, *Juliet of the Spirits*, *La Dolce Vita*.

'I'm not looking my best.' I passed a hand through my dyed blond hair with its black roots.

'I don't think O'Toole is still looking like Lawrence of Arabia.'

And that was how I stumbled off the plane at Rome International, in a paisley shirt, beads, an ankh and black roots. The great man was there to meet me and it was love at first sight.

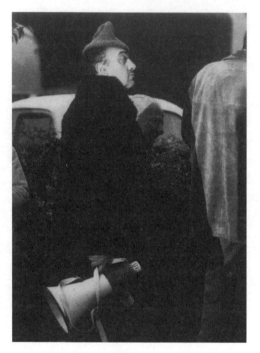

Maestro Fellini – say no more

He'd accepted the gig of three of Edgar Allan Poe's short stories. There were to be three directors, Buñuel, Bergman and himself. He'd spent his advance immediately.

When the producers announced they hadn't got Bergman or Buñuel they said, 'But we've got you, so let's go'. O'Toole had had the script for a week when Fellini's phone rang late at night. O'Toole's dramatic voice came down the line:

'I don't want to play the part. I'm a bastard. Goodbye.'

'I guess I'd hit a nerve.'

'It's well known he likes the sherbet.'

'Zee sherbet?'

'The booze. Mike Caine understudied him in his first West End play, The Long and the Short and the Tall. Caine told me it was really frustrating. O'Toole would arrive just before curtain up, drunk as a lord, throw on his costume, rub his hands along the dusty theatre walls en route to the stage, smearing the grime onto his face as he waited in the wings. When his feet hit the boards, however, he became stone-cold sober, justifying the rave reviews he'd received from the critics. The foremost was Kenneth Tynan, who never forgot his portrayal of Private Bamforth. Yet Tynan stated publicly that he was never the same actor after his nose job. A requirement

O'Toole felt was necessary to become the film star he became after David Lean's masterwork hit the screen.'

Fellini didn't let me return to London. He checked me into the Hotel Inghilterra for the first week, from where we spent the days hanging out at his favourite haunts. During the second week he took me to meet his wife, Giulietta Masina. I assume they decided I should move out of the Inghilterra and into the guest room of their Fregene home. She became the second actress that I considered a great creative artist and studied close up. It was a wondrous experience for me to spend time with the woman who'd inspired the creation of the musical *Sweet Charity*, as I have never seen a performance of it that reached into Charity's heart the way that Giulietta did.

Most nights after I had gone to bed my door would ease open, and they would look in to make sure I was alright.

A few days before shooting began, Fellini explained to me that he had no time to spend with me and thought that I should move back into the hotel to be on hand for all the last-minute costume, make-up and hair meetings some of his troupe would need. As I spoke no Italian and they little English, he would arrange a translator to be by my side.

That was how Patrizia Bachelet came into my life. And a valuable addition she became too. You could say it was in the stars. Our initial outing together was to a hair salon to affix a curious distortion to one of my eyebrows, which the director had masterminded on my behalf.

Trying to get extra insight into what prompted Fellini's inspirations, I asked Patrizia about the twisted eyebrow. She took a moment, then said, 'He explained: "It's a question mark." He rarely tells all.' Yeah, I thought, he doesn't want to limit what the audience get for themselves.

Another great treat of *Toby Dammit* (Fellini's title for the piece) was becoming a colleague of Piero Tosi, who at the time was considered to be the very finest costume designer in the European industry. He seemed to understand and appreciate my interest in his craft, and while it couldn't be considered a stretch for him to conceive how best Toby should be turned out, he took it upon himself to introduce me to the craftsmen he'd selected over the years to implement his visions.

Some of the clothes I had made during that time, and later when residing in the Eternal City, I still wear today. The most treasured was the pure linen pink suit without lining that his tailor cut for me in 1968. Before I had had the occasion to wear it myself, my sibling Christopher Thomas 'borrowed' it from my chambers in the Albany to launch his production of *Tommy* at Cannes. Word reached me during the production of *Teorema* via my new Italian agent Ibrahim Moussa, who was also at Cannes that year.

'Ah Terri', he announced in his thick Egyptian accent, 'your brother's suit, amazing, all the festival was gossiping about it!'

'My brother Chris?'

'Yeah. What a guy. And a PINK suit, nobody had ever seen anything like it!'

I telephoned my Aunt Maude, who doubled as my secretary-housekeeper.

'Maude. Did you let Chris have my pink suit?'

'Er … I did.'

'Maude. Why on earth? You knew I was keeping it for something special.'

A pause.

'Well, you know what he's like.'

Indeed I did.

When I accosted him face to face he responded, 'Well, I had it cleaned and pressed before I got it back to Maude.'

Yeah, right, Chris. He's not considered the sharpest of Tom and Ethel's progeny for nothing.

The rent of the chambers in Albany was reasonable enough for me to consider them as a perfect base. I took my time making it a lifestyle that I could return to between jobs. And whenever I fell in love with a foreign country I never felt in a rush to return home; Albany was being perfected with or without my presence. Very few stayed there in my absence and the few that did were always under Maude's auspices. Slowly other residents appeared to accept me and befriend me. Even Edward Heath, after he became the Prime Minister, invited me to lunch, where he confided in me his ideas to prise the UK into the Common Market in spite of the fact I told him it would never work. Brits are leaders, not followers, I admonished. In retrospect he wasn't a man who took notice of anyone, least of all me.

10

'I'd like to meet that young man.'

Krishnamurti to Fellini on seeing footage of *Toby Dammit*

Are you a believer in the theory that great events happen in threes? I guess during my initial sojourn in Rome I took it on board. The first: Fellini, not only meeting him and learning from the man and his wife, and everything inferred by that, but their unconditional acceptance of me, which gave me added inner strength.

This first situation gave rise to the second when Patrizia, my interpreter, drew my attention to the fact that a man, an extraordinary man, from her obvious respect of him, came into the orbit of my own life. Patrizia turned out to be an astrologer, Fellini's astrologer in fact. She later completed a chart for yours truly. She also had a chum with the impressive name and title of Contessa Vanda Passigli-Scaravelli. Patrizia had often referred to her friend as Vanda, and promised to introduce us. I gathered she'd decided it was time, as I was invited to a lunch that Vanda was about to give. I didn't know the half of it. Nevertheless, Patrizia informed me several times that a gentleman named Krishnamurti would be present. When I failed to respond with suitable interest, even awe, she reiterated: 'Krishnamurti. He's a sage!'

Now I don't expect you to believe me when I tell you that my only knowledge of the word was as the name for an ingredient in the Christmas turkey: the sage and onion stuffing. It was apparent Patrizia intended me to attend this lunch and I must confess I had no intention of missing it. I only wanted to wind her up a little to get more background on what I was being included in.

The time arrived. Lunch, actually. It was a large gathering. Stringers from *Time* and *Newsweek* asked questions of the slight figure sat opposite

Jeddu Krishnamurti

me at one of the separate tables in the spacious room. Yet even at the moment I was seated opposite the sage, I considered my presence happenstance. I don't recall any of the questions put or any of the unflustered answers given.

'How do you understand "sage"?' I had asked Patrizia.

'A person who has wisdom. Embodies it.'

The gentleman sat opposite was delicate, fine featured. By the light coffee colour of his skin, Indian. As he was primarily occupied with the journalists' enquiries, I was able to study him. It was only when the food arrived, totally vegetarian, that I became aware I was staring when he glanced at me and lowered his eyes as if to shield himself. His eyelashes were black and the longest I'd ever seen on a man. We didn't speak. When the meal was finished everyone got up, the chairs and tables were pushed aside and there was a general milling around. I didn't notice Krishnamurti leave the room. A short while later a middle-aged guy introduced himself.

'My name is Alan Nodé. I am Krishnaji's secretary. Would you like to accompany him on his afternoon walk?' I nodded. And his secretary guided me to the back of the building where the slight figure waited. Did I mention how elegantly dressed he was?

The area immediately around the building was open yet nondescript, unlike the Rome I'd become accustomed to. We walked. If during the lunch I'd been lost for words, I made up for it now, chattering endlessly. I recall telling him of my Uncle John, a Jesuit monk in Australia, who had a near-death experience while in hospital.

At a certain point he stopped walking, half turned to face me, and said: 'Look at that tree.'

I did. Hardly a tree at all. A sapling struggling to stay upright amidst the inhospitable landscape.

I turned my look at him. He returned it. We continued walking. I continued rambling on. After a further ten minutes or so he again stopped and turning again to me and looking up, said: 'Look at that cloud.'

Slowly I complied. A cloud. Nothing special, grey, commonplace in fact. A pause. I looked back at him. He smiled, a very small smile. We came walking back from where we had set off.

I wish I could tell you some profound realisation had occurred, but no. It wasn't until much time had passed that I realised something profound had happened; it was too subtle for me to comprehend at the time.

Vanda Scaraveli, my first yoga teacher

Changes did happen, however. My contentment with the outer trappings of success no longer seemed to satisfy me. I asked Patrizia to get me closer to Krishnamurti's friend Contessa Vanda Passigli-Scaravelli. On Patrizia's urging I gave up eating meat and fish. Contessa Vanda gave me my initial breathing lessons and under her guidance I took up yoga.

It turned out that Krishnamurti and Vanda had only begun doing yoga themselves a few years back. On returning from one of his yearly sojourns in India he had announced: 'We must start doing yoga. I've studied the people who practice and their bodily health does improve.' He became a student of TKV Desikachar. And soon began inviting the esteemed teachers of yoga to visit him and Vanda during the Swiss summer talks in Saanen – Desikachar, Krishnamacharya and Inenga. And it was only after he was injured during a workout with Inenga that he invited Vanda to teach him herself. She had apparently really taken to the yogic asanas. Although she had reservations, Krishnamurti convinced her. 'You're the only one who doesn't hurt me', he insisted. And that's how my first forays into the ancient science were given at the hands of Krishnamurti's chosen teacher.

11

Bitter Rice revisited.

During one of my last strolls around the Eternal City, I was at the Spanish-Steps-end of Via Condotti when I espied Piero Tosi with his great chum Roberto Coppa. They were a trio, yet I didn't recognise their female companion until they came closer.

Since my initial visits to the cinema, first with my mother, and then as soon as I was old enough by myself, I had developed a fairly unerring choice

Brando

of films and their featured players. Initially the male stars influenced my selections. As the price of the tickets was my own responsibility, my discernment developed in haste. Cooper, Clift, Brando, Dean, Lancaster became staples. The ladies were rarer. Yet one impinged herself on my psyche so completely I can recall it like yesterday. I had made the trip up west on a Saturday afternoon to a small snug arthouse cinema in Tottenham Court Road. I guess

I must have been around fourteen years old, so it was still quite an adventure. The poster for the movie had caught my eye. I boarded the District Line at Plaistow and changed on to the Central at Mile End. The title: *Bitter Rice*. And I was touched by Silvana Mangano in a much more adult fashion than by Gene Tierney or Hedy Lamarr. The girls at Plaistow Grammar, my own age, only had eyes for the prefects, older guys in the sixth form, as though they had ideas that I didn't. Yet initially it was older women who first found me attractive, and I benefitted greatly from their mature expertise. And without putting too much of a romantic spin on things, it may have been the cravings that I felt for Silvana Mangano emanating from my being that older women picked up on.

Anyway, the initially unrecognised female with Piero and Roberto was none other than the *Bitter Rice* heroine of my dreams, in the flesh. And what flesh it was too. So overwhelmed was I by the realisation that I felt a bit unsteady on my feet yet was revived by the aroma that enveloped me. The very first time I had inhaled the fragrance of Tuber Rose.

I could hear Piero introducing us, but for a change it was my eyelids that were lowered when subjected to the inky steadiness of her scrutiny. The early zaftig of her teenage frame was no longer in evidence, the svelte line of her body complimented by the high-fashion two-piece that embraced it. She was saying to Tosi in Italian: 'He would be perfect in Pier Paolo's film.' And then to me in English: 'Do you know Pier Paolo Pasolini?' I stammered something. 'I know his work, not the man.'

'He's about to start work on his next. It's called *Teorema*.'

Her English was perfect. There was a low catch in her delivery, which great sound engineers could catch with an up-close microphone.

I heard myself saying, or rather drooling, 'Are you in it?'

Then I saw the smile for the first time, as if the question had unexpectedly amused her. 'Yes. Of course.'

As a result of the wonderfully fleeting moment in Via Condotti, Pasolini and Franco Rossellini, the nephew of Roberto Rossellini, came to London to talk to me. We met at Claridges Hotel. Pasolini was small and wiry, Rossellini tall and bendy. The director didn't speak English and his producer translated for him. Pasolini outlined his subject: 'It concerns a petit bourgeois family in Milan. Father, mother, son, daughter, and a maid. Into their lives appears a stranger. He has a divine nature. He makes love to all the family and the maid, and then leaves. This would be your part.'

'I can do that', I said.

While I was waiting to get my marching orders to report in Milan, two memorable things occurred: I heard that Rita Hayworth was in London and I figured the concierge at the Connaught would know where she usually stayed. I dropped by.

'She's staying with us, sir. Shall I connect you?'

Shot by Anthony Armstrong Jones, about the time I worked with Pasolini

I took a few full breaths.

'Hello. My name is Terence Stamp. I've always hoped to meet you. Are you free for supper while you're in town?'

I took her to Parks in Beauchamp Place. I knew the chef-owner Tom Benson. He put us in the kitchen, which had a small table he kept for chums.

12

'Dogs look up to you. Cats look down on you. But pigs – thems is equals.'

Frederik Van Pallandt

In April 1962 I had been interviewed for the *Daily Express* by their star showbiz journalist Herbert Kretzmer. He was an imposing, handsome man who made elegant use of spoken English, albeit being born in South Africa. I was flattered the paper had sent him as I had only just got out of the blocks. It was my first real interview apart from the press conference that Ustinov had used to launch the start of his film *Billy Budd*. It was easy to get along with Mr Kretzmer and I assumed this was the case with everyone he interviewed. Yet when our chat was finished and I was seeing him out of the little mews where I was staying, he said, 'I'm usually at the *Express* building in Fleet Street. If you're in the area call in, we'll have a coffee, I'll show you around.' A few weeks later I did just that, and we've been friends ever since.

While I was waiting to begin *Teorema* with Silvana and Pasolini in Milan, Herbie took me to meet another of his chums: Frederik, the male half of the singing duo Nina and Frederik. Herbie told me a little of Frederik as we strolled to the apartment on Embankment Gardens. I got the impression Herbie had enormous respect for the gentleman we were about to meet. The Dutch Frederik Van Pallandt was also a very tall guy and I felt quite small between them in the modest studio Frederik had made for a little privacy in their family home with his wife and three kids. The studio was compact yet the high ceilings were pronounced by the low tables; we sat on the carpeted floor. There were no pictures on the walls, yet the wall which ran the depth of the room housed floor-to-ceiling books. A set of these in marigold yellows were entitled *The Sufi Message*, twelve volumes.

Frederik himself was a handsome guy, well over six feet (6'3" or 4"). What became apparent almost immediately was his grace of movement, not seen too often in men. This really came home to me after the Nordic beauty Nina brought us refreshment, served us and left the tray on the low table where her husband was seated. Frederik owned a farm in Spain, and he and Herbie were discussing Herbie's meetings with both of the great matadors Antonio Ordoñez and Luis Miguel Dominguín, and how he had asked them both about their fear while in the hotel awaiting the confrontation in the bullring: Ordoñez had commented, 'The bull isn't in the hotel', while Dominguín responded that on the afternoons of a fight he felt a different kind of fear, a spiritual fear unlike anything else. Which he felt he needed. 'It is like waking up after being asleep too long. I come alive.'

Frederik was intrigued and asked Herbie who he felt was the more alert during the interviews.

I don't recall the answer, as my attention became suddenly focused on the table in front of Frederik on which sat the remnants of our snack. Frederik was also observing it intently; he then quickly moved a few of the objects, altering their position on the surface. Yet I could not fail to notice the shift from the random array into a harmonious setting, actually not unlike a still life composition, except in a living dimension; as if a Calder had dropped onto his table. My God, I thought, the guy has more than a physical grace. He didn't appear to even notice my witnessing of it.

Frederik continued his conversation with Herbie. 'Had Dominguín defined this shift in attention?' It was as though his artistic conception on the table was so commonplace it passed without undue notice. On reflection, I realised it was commonplace to him. Herbie, replying to Frederik, quoted: 'The danger, the acute physical risk, cleared his mind and brought him closer to himself.' As on fight days, which could be his last day on Earth, to live this life he needed an imperative motivation, not something to do, but something he must do.

As we were leaving, Frederik saw me looking at the yellow hardbacks at eye-level in the bookshelf. 'They are something my father got together, taken from an important man's talks. We'll discuss them next time. Give me a ring: Flaxman One thousand.'

Hazrat Inayat Khan with his beloved Vina

Which is how an important friendship that was to encompass some of the unexpected changes in my life, began.

There were similarities in the friendship that happened between Frederik and me to the friendship between my brother Chris and his pal and partner Kit Lambert. Kit couldn't have been more upper-class, his public-school education and sophisticated upbringing were the opposite of my brother's. Kit was gay, which Chris definitely wasn't, yet they were as harmonious as the C and G keys on a piano. It was a case of 2 and 2 making 5. Or even 7, judging by the deals they did with record companies, benchmarks still admired by performing musical acts today.

On the surface, Frederik and I had things in common. We were both in the entertainment industry, for example, yet I don't recall any of our early hanging out sessions talking about show business. His title – he was a Baron – stretched back hundreds of years. As his mother was Countess

Else Blücher-Altona (from the Blücher who defeated Napoleon with Wellington), Frederik qualified for the Four Quarters Club, whose members were confined to individuals whose all four grandparents had held titles.

I can't say what he got out of our friendship, yet for me he embodied a refinement I yearned for yet was unaware of until he came into my life on the Embankment.

Whilst he professed to have little input into the stage act he and Nina performed – 'She's the voice, I just fill in with chat' – he did have a profound interest in breath. For me, the breath is the voice. He once demonstrated a practice he'd invented whereby while blowing a note on a wooden flute he could simultaneously inhale without interruption to the note being played. He credited his interest in breath to his father, the Baron Floris, who had studied with Hazrat Inayat Khan, whose books he'd overseen. He was particularly interested in sound. He had an old clock in his studio and conversation would often be put on hold whenever it chimed. He said it was to remind him to pause his thoughts to listen completely to the 'Hu'. I never managed his uninterrupted whistle practice, but I did get to meet his father, the keeper of Inayat Khan's breath secrets.

One of my early screen idols was Cary Grant, and when I discovered he started life in a poor district of Bristol my appreciation intensified. If only I could get to talk to him and find out as to exactly how he'd made the transformation. I had my chance when I caught sight of him in Old Burlington Street just before I went off to start *Teorema*. Yet in that moment my confidence deserted me. I felt too overwhelmed to accost him. But I took in everything I could. He was impossibly handsome in the flesh and extremely well turned out. I had the definite sense that he dressed primarily for Cary. His shoes, three quarter brogues, were made-to-measure and set him sure-footed where he stood. They were shiny yet not intrusive and looked comfortable. Of course no one who'd run away from home as a teenager to become the top-boy in a circus tumbling act would be unaware of the importance of his feet, not just how they looked.

Some years later I was visiting in St James and saw a raincoat in the window of Aquascutum; it was pink. I went in to get a close-up. Slipping it on, I quizzed the assistant.

'Have you sold any of these?'

'Yes, sir. We have sold one.'

'Only one. You sure?'

'Yes, sir. Cary Grant purchased it.'

'I'll take it.'

It is still worn today, albeit causing less of a stir in these times of pushy pinks.

Contessa Vanda, my very first yoga teacher, was always appropriately turned out, yet even on occasions, including in the well-dressed society of Rome and Florence, Vanda only wore her rubber flip-flops. More mindful of the importance of her feet than how they looked. She never criticised my footwear, but it was only a matter of time as my own feet became more yoga-ised that open sandals became the norm, with my Cleverleys reserved for special events.

One of those very special events was the blind date with Brigitte Bardot, which my agent, the loveable Jimmy Fraser, had arranged with her agent, Olga Horstig Primuz. I immediately became self-conscious about my hair, which I was allowing to grow out from its *Toby Dammit* peroxide clobbering. I rang  a new chum, Vidal Sassoon, who I had met when I was with Jean Shrimpton.

'Listen, Vidal, I need a favour: could you cut my barnet yourself?'

Vidal was a fellow East Ender. We'd both arrived in this world within the sound of Bow Bells.

I duly reported to his flat at the Park-Lane-end of Curzon Street. When I was precariously perched on the side of his bath, he enquired:

'So, what's so special?'

'I've got a date with BB. Fly to Paris tomorrow.'

'You're kidding.'

'Nope.'

'That's special.'

'For some reason, I'm nervous. I'm assuming she's seen me in a movie. You know I don't look as good in the flesh.'

'Maybe she feels the same. What are you going to wear?'

'I haven't thought about it.'

'Well, first impressions and all that ... '

'Yeah.'

'OK, let's give you a proper trim to start. Short and horny. OK.'

It was a smart idea Vidal had, always elegant himself. What should I wear? Not too studied, not too casual. What would Mr Grant have done? I'm certain he'd faced this situation more times than yours truly. When I'd caught sight of him in St James his style was, or appeared, effortless. Of course he dressed primarily for himself.

What did I want, no, need, for my debut in Paris? The afternoon before my early evening flight I had a flash. What was currently in my wardrobe that I felt most comfortable wearing? The answer was the old drop-falls strides I had worn on the *Madding Crowd* shoot. I'd felt so comfortable I'd made sure they'd ended up with me when the shoot ended. They apparently were always cut on the easy side to accommodate the curious design: two sides which contain the pocket construction which, when fastened by three central buttons, are concealed by a flap which does up just below where they are braced up. This flap has four buttons too, one each side of the centre and one at each end. These are generally left unbuttoned for easy access to the now concealed pocket.

My taxi arrived at the given address. I was taken aback by the size of the gathering. A party in progress, in fact. Yet, of course, very sophisticated, very French. The avoidance of one-to-one introduction. I espied her across the room. Casually dressed. In slacks so I couldn't gape at the fabulous legs I gaped at on the screen so often. The irrepressible bottom defied disguise.

Olga introduced herself and took me across the room; the early prequel of computer dating. And there she was! The eyes which needed no enhancement, were carefully enhanced. The lips, which certainly needed no lipstick, criminally crimson. She smiled. And God created woman, indeed.

We chatted stiltedly, with her agent helping out. I regretted having wasted the five years at Plaistow Grammar not learning French. I felt decidedly unsophisticated. Olga politely drifted away. We were left alone. Silence. I must have put my hands thoughtlessly in my trouser pockets. She must have noticed and pointed to my now concealed hands.

'What is zith?' she enquired, pointing to the flap of my drop-fall strides.

Galvanised, I grasped her outstretched fingers. I drew them theatrically toward the flap.

'I have a little mouse in here', I said.

13

'When an individual becomes a person, the beauty hidden in the individual, which is divine, develops; and that development of beauty is personality.'

Hazrat Inayat Khan

On my way to Milan for the start of *Teorema*, Frederik thought it timely to go via The Hague to meet his Dad.

Floris was a tall, imposing man with an aristocratic head, as well he might, as he was a Baron and his ancestors the Van Pallandts stretched back centuries. The Baron was the Dutch Ambassador to France at the outbreak of World War II, only leaving the embassy when the Nazis were entering Paris. However, as soon the conflict was over, the family returned and Floris came upon a flybill that was to alter his life, announcing a talk on Sufism by one Hazrat Inayat Khan. Previously having had no interest in philosophy, he was drawn by the word he'd not encountered before, 'Sufism'.

Hazrat, his younger brother Musharaf and his cousin Ali had been dispatched from India by their guru to bring the message to the West. On arrival in France, without any visible means of support yet all being muso's (Hazrat's grandfather was considered the Beethoven of India), they found musical employment as Mata Hari's backing group.

Hazrat played the vina, known locally as struck music. The vina is given a special place in India, as it is considered to be most akin to the human voice. Only after his enlightenment did he cease to play, saying: 'I gave up my music because I had received from it all that I had to receive. To serve God one must sacrifice what is dearest to one; and so I sacrificed my music. I had arrived at a stage where I touched the Music of the Spheres. Then every soul became for me a musical note, and all life became music. Now, if I do anything, it is to tune souls instead of instruments.'

'It's very nice to meet any friend of my son, now what can I do for you?'

'Frederik said you were the keeper of the papers for Murshid Khan.'

'That's correct, he entrusted them to me to formulate into some volumes of *The Sufi Message*. Is there anything especial you're interested in?'

'Breath. The breath. I understand he knew a great deal about the breath.'

He did. The problem is his lectures on breath were usually esoterica, for a few *mureeds* (pupils), and he was aware how breath could be damaging if incorrectly practiced. His instructions were as much about rhythm as anything else. Also it wasn't a part of his teaching that was for the general public. His pupils were encouraged not to discuss esoteric matters, which are so easily misunderstood. Even a soul as beautiful as Jesus was criticised for talking of the inherent glory within us all.

There followed a silence. It wasn't uncomfortable.

'I understand you've met Jiddu Krishnamurti.'

'Yes.'

'How did that come to pass?'

'Federico Fellini showed him some rushes of a film we were shooting when he came to Rome. He asked to meet me.'

'Did he indeed. And ... '

'He keeps an eye on me. I see him once a year maybe. He's so austere, I can't follow a lot of what he says.'

'Yes. He does talk a lot about what it isn't. Yet I hear he is exquisite in person.'

'Lit from within, is how he felt to me, that first time.'

'Yes. I know that feeling.'

Another long moment passed. And then he smiled.

'I suppose I can trust someone who Krishnamurti is keeping an eye on. Repeat after me, it's a kind of *wazifa*, something Murshid had us repeat at the start of any talk: "Toward the One, the perfection of Love,

Harmony and Beauty. The Only Being united with all the illuminated Souls who form the embodiment of the Master, the Spirit of Guidance." Now tell me more of why you want to study the breath.'

'I'm a performer, I studied voice at drama school, yet no one specialised in breathing and I had troubles with the poetic passages in Shakespeare. So I was drawn to the phenomenon of breath. Vanda Scaravelli, who teaches Krishnamurti yoga, has instructed me with the *asanas* but seems reluctant to go deeply into breathing or pass on what she knows. Krishnamurti doesn't refer to breathing at all. I think that creative artists can regard themselves as athletes. It all begins with breath, doesn't it? And nobody seems to give it any thought.'

'You're right. Murshid said: "A man who has not gained power over his breath is like a king who has no power over his domain." It is different in India, both the Brahmin and the Sufis teach their children about complete breath when they are nine years old. It gives them a fuller life in every way. Murshid told me that metaphysically every person has a certain degree of life in them which can be distinguished by his or her breath. And that degree shows itself to the seer as colour, yet even those who have not attained that power of perception can perceive it in a person's voice. If you practice complete breathing regularly your voice will naturally develop to its fullest potential.'

'I hope this doesn't sound silly, yet Kristnamurti has what I think of as a bearing of being. If I could aspire to that it would bring to my work an effortlessness.'

'We will discuss what Murshid told us as a group and all your questions will become clear. You can make notes today, but later let's see what you recall. OK?'

'OK.'

'It helps to develop listening, just listening; when Murshid came to the West he told me the unstruck music remained with him, even as he was in the roaring streets of Manhattan. The breath will enable you to a different quality of listening.'

'What are Sufis?'

'You could say they are to Islam what Zen is to Buddhism. They are the esoteric aspect that develops the one within them. Jelal-a-Din Rumi was one of the earliest known masters to practice Sufism. He is considered the Shakespeare of Persia, the originator of the Whirling

Dervishes. It is said the order of Whirling Dervish was based upon his moment of enlightenment when in the ecstasy embodied he turned a full circle in wonderment and his robe left the impression of a circle in the dust where he turned. He was a thirteenth-century poet, yet the dervish order flourishes still.

'One of the first practices Murshid gave to me he called a *Fikar*, and this is what I am going to pass on to you. The breath is like a swing which has a continual motion, and whatever is put in the swing swings also with the movement of the breath. *Fikar*, therefore, is not a breathing practice. In *Fikar* it is not necessary that one should breathe in a certain way, different from one's usual breathing. *Fikar* is becoming conscious of the natural movement of the breath and, picturing breath as a swing, putting in that swing a certain thought, as a babe in a cradle, to rock it. Only the difference in the rocking is that it is an intentional activity on the part of the person who rocks the cradle, and in *Fikar* no effort must be made to change the rhythms of the breath, the breath must be left to its own usual rhythm. One need not try even to regulate the rhythm of the breath,

Learning to Whirl

for the whole mechanism of one's body is already working rhythmically, so the breath is rhythmical by nature, and it is the very breath itself which causes man to distinguish rhythm.

'What is important in *Fikar* is not the rhythm, but the concentration. *Fikar* is swinging the concentrated thought with the movement of the breath, for breath is life and it gives life to the thought, which is repeated with the breath. On the rhythm of the breath, the circulation of the blood and the pulsation of the heart and head depend, which means that the whole mechanism of the body, also of the mind, is directed by the rhythm of the breath. When a thought is attached to the breath by concentration, then the effect of that thought reaches every atom of one's mind and body. Plainly speaking, the thought held in *Fikar* runs with the circulation of the blood through every vein and tube of the body, and the influence of the thought is spread through every faculty of the mind. Therefore the reaction of the *Fikar* is the resonance of the same thought expressing itself through one's thought, speech and action. So in time the thought one holds in *Fikar* becomes the reality of one's self.

'For a Sufi, therefore, breath is a key to concentration. The Sufi, so to speak, puts his thought under the cover of the breath. This expression of Rumi's I would interpret as meaning that the Sufi lays his beloved ideal in the swing of the breath.

'I feel that's enough for now. Oh, Frederik tells me you have a set in the Albany. Does Graham Greene still reside there?'

'I'm not sure. Everyone keeps themselves to themselves.'

'My wife and I will be making a trip to London next month, God willing, we can look you up if you like.'

'Yes, that will be great.'

'I'll bring some of Murshid's papers, we can go over them.'

As I went to stand up, he stopped me.

'Get used to standing up without using your arms, it strengthens your core. The organs used in the respiratory process need to be made strong before we can work on the more delicate aspects of the breath's magnetism. You'll be surprised how many times you sit down and get up during a day. It's a good way to start accommodating your practices into everyday life, tops up your awareness. I've enjoyed meeting you, see you in London. Tea at the Albany.'

'Tea at the Albany. Inshallah!'

'Inshallah!

Principe di Savoia was one of Milan's best hotels, and grand it was too. Italian luxury is luxurious. Every possible consideration for their guests to be made comfortable had been implemented. I could really become used to this, I thought, but Pasolini didn't waste any time and his method of shooting was as quick as Ken Loach, and equally as spontaneous. The part of the Guest, mine, was almost without dialogue and he offered me no direction. Yet after a few days I became aware that he was operating a hand-held camera himself and appeared to be turning over on me when I was unaware he was shooting. Initially I wasn't sure, yet it became evident it was the case. This was more off-the-cuff than the *Poor Cow* shoot and it became a game for me to let him think I was unaware when I wasn't. I did, however, come to the conclusion he was looking for an impromptu happening, unlike usual performing. Not unlike Anthony Newley's 'doing nothing' advice, yet not like 'nothing doing' of reality TV. As Cary Grant once told a chum of mine, 'When it looks so simple, so relaxed, like Picasso, Hammerstein, all confidence and command, but it is really the eventual distillation of all experience.'

I must confess to eagerly awaiting my kiss with Silvana. It is interesting, an actor's relationship with his leading ladies. If you don't love them, and are meant to, you have to find something loveable about them and keep it in mind, and the opposite also applies. Up until *Teorema* my leading ladies weren't unknown to me, so the aforementioned situations presented no problem. With *Teorema*, Silvana in particular, it was a new role I'd been cast in. The 'divine nature' of the guest was Pasolini's creation, and as he rarely spoke to me personally I had no help in that direction. My fellow artists spoke little or no English and the manifestation of the divine nature was a subject I wasn't about to discuss with even my best chums. In this sense I was alone in Milan. Silvana had an English

Michael Stevenson

mother, alive and well in Rome. Her father was a Sicilian, no longer with us. I had little opportunity to get to know Silvana before our love scene and most of what I knew about her life had been furnished by my agent in Italy, Ibrahim Moussa. Her early marriage, before she was twenty, to film producer Dino de Laurentis was a mystery in showbiz circles. He was extremely small in stature and not what you would call physically attractive. The sort of powerful film producer a would-be starlet would set her cap at, yet Silvana was the hottest property of the day before she met him. She had four children, a son and three daughters, the eldest of which was married and had a child of her own. Silvana would have been around forty-five at the time, and a grandmother.

I just had to await the day. I got myself into the all-seeing frame of mind by imagining how it must have been for Christ, who had proclaimed himself a keynote in harmony with every soul. A fact that ended with his crucifixion. The scenes with the father, daughter, son and maid all went fine. The day of the kiss dawned. We only had one take. I am not sure if my intensity shocked Silvana when our lips met, but it was over all too soon. Yet it lingered long in memory, embellished by the tuber-rose aroma that clouded about her.

14

The lull begins

The Mind of Mr Soames was a film I made in 1969. It was, I thought, an unusual, interesting screenplay. It went well, my first job still on the high of making *Teorema* and *Toby Dammit*. Even if I had a crystal ball I would have found it hard to believe this was to be my last leading part in

an English-speaking studio film for almost ten years. I was thirty-one, in good shape, you could say in my prime. Yet it's hard to understand the machinations of the workings of the Universe. This was to be the beginning of my lull.

Most performers who have a long career have a lull. Sometimes it happens at the start: Humphrey Bogart didn't get a lead until he was forty-two, Jack Nicholson didn't get his break until he was thirty, the age when mine was to begin. Even the superb Cary Grant had a lull in the middle years. Of course I didn't know any of this when it happened to me. No offers. No work. Weeks became

The Mind of Mr Soames

months, months years. Jimmy Fraser sounded increasingly embarrassed whenever I checked in. Before cash dried up I travelled to Italy to study with Vanda. In London I attended Krishnamurti's lectures, hoping to derive a philosophical solution to my woes.

'When the eagle flies it leaves no mark' didn't help. 'The observer is the observed' didn't either. I never questioned Krishnamurti's authenticity, assumed it was my thickness that was the problem. One day I thought:

Why don't I start further down the ladder? I sold some of my antiques, the Chateau d'Yquem I'd invested in. Put the proceeds into my Mum and Dad's bank account. Purchased a round-the-world ticket. Carefully packed my weekend Gucci holdall and set off. First stop: Delhi. My friend Frederik felt my trip to be a good idea.

'It'll broaden your outlook, but remember there are thousands of charlatans to every bright one. Though the women are gorgeous, not more gorgeous than here, it's just there are more of them, many more of them.'

'Do you speak any Indian, Frederik?'

'No, everyone there speaks English, better English than you, probably.'

'Better than me? How come?'

'They studied English. You just picked it up. Believe me, you'll be surprised. The people you'll be hoping to meet will all speak English.'

As it turned out, that wasn't the case, but I will get into that later.

I recall making an effort at least at the start of my journey to practice the smiling forehead of the Sufis. If you are curious to know of a smiling forehead other than in a Rumi poem, check out the actress Jo Lumley or even just listen to her voice. She's not only a poem, yet a poem as well: a poem in motion.

Once settled in the hotel in Delhi, I headed off to pay my respects at the tomb of Hazrat Inayat Khan. However, when I arrived at the Nizamuddin Awlia Corner I realised someone had beaten me to it. An older gentleman in a heavily patched robe was contemplating with his head bowed. He must have sensed my arrival as he raised his head and glanced in my direction.

'Excuse me', I said.

'It's open to everyone. That's how Murshid would have had it', he answered.

'Did you know Murshid Inayat?'

'Knew his grandfather. The composer.'

'Ah!' A pause. 'Are you a Sufi?'

'Yes. Dervish in travelling order.' He indicated his patched robe.

'What's the symbolism of the patches?'

He grinned. 'That the robe's got holes. I suppose the fact that we travel minus luggage and need to borrow a needle and thread, as we sew on our patches, is the significance. As most dervishes sew on their own patches. Is this your first excursion to the East?'

'Yes, is it that obvious?'

He smiled again. It was warm, welcoming.

'I've studied Murshid Kahn's books.'

'You'll find it is different actually being here.'

'Already. I've felt like a stranger in a strange land.'

'Ah! Like Moses. Well, he did OK I suppose.'

As an apparent afterthought he added: 'There's an old man located somewhere near here who knows a rare but interesting *zikr*. He's only known locally as Sufi Sahib. I am sure you could locate him. Do you know the prayers?'

'I'm afraid not.'

'Oh, well, there is a moment for everything. Hazr ba kadam.'

'Wozzat?'

'It's something said when an enclave of dervishes are out walking together. One of them takes it upon himself to remind the group to stay aware. It means "Look and remember whose feet are walking". There are two shadows. One that is projected upon the sky and another which falls upon the ground, the former known to the mystic and the latter to everyone. Goodbye. Marshalla!'

'Marshalla.'

Frederik joined me in Delhi. It had been his idea. He had only just wound up an engagement, with Nina, at the Albert Hall, and was evidently taking a leisurely route to Japan to discuss a brief yet profitable season there. I told him of my encounter with the gent in the patched robe and his tip about Sufi Sahib.

15

The Qalb zikr

Initially it was the Baron who was more intrigued, as he understood the rare zikr had been practiced in Egypt and convinced himself Napoleon had encountered the practice during his Egyptian campaign when a lowly soldier in the French army, returning to become the Emperor we remember today. His portal to power, the Qalb zikr.

Our choice of a place to crash was the weird and wonderful Lodhi Hotel, which on arrival we retitled the Lodhi Prison. It was, however, a stone's throw from the Nizamuddin Awlia Corner where Murshid Hazrat Inayat Khan was entombed, and we were able to pay our silent respects to him.

In those days, Sufi resting places or dargas were considered to be locations of spiritual emanations, and lots of Muslims meditated, even lived on site, and it was there at the famous corner we finally heard about the location of Sufi Sahib, the keeper of the Qalb zikr.

Early the next morning we set off, by bus, to the deprived area that borders the Delhi University. And whilst we had no specific directions, amongst the vulture-inhabited wasteland we came upon a contingent of Nissan huts, and sitting outside one on a dining-room chair was a formidable hook-nosed gent who looked for all the world like the fictional character Nasruddin, of Sufi legend.

The Baron and I exchanged a glance: 'This has to be our man'.

Frederik was an unusually erudite fella and his natural grace extended to his way with words. He also spoke about ten languages fluently. And having spent some of his boyhood in India at the Dutch Embassy, he found it easy to communicate with the locals. However, Sufi Sahib was comfortable with English and Frederik explained our quest. The turbaned venerable didn't seem fazed by his incongruous visitors, and while he would never have admitted it, I think he was quite tickled to meet a couple of mureeds who had travelled such a long way to receive instruction.

We were soon sitting on the floor of his meagre accommodation. He was a practicing Muslim as well as a Sufi. 'This is the only bindi I have', he once said, indicating a callous in the middle of his forehead: the spot that was grounded during the regular prayers that had measured off his life.

Prayerful Muslim he may have been, yet taking in the bare necessities of his existence he appeared more like a fakir to me.

Instruction began straight away as he explained the complexities of encouraging the heart to speak or vibrate in rhythm. Using our tasbis we began with la illa ha illala, all the while focussing our attention on the psychic centre of the heart, on the right side of the chest, in this case.

As the days passed and our visits to Sufi Sahib became a regular part of our routine, this concentration on a point in the body tended to make the mind one-pointed and our hearts started to resonate with spoken or thought zikr, Frederik's the day before my own. When this occurred the old dervish instructed us to move the resonance to the left side of the chest and soon to the middle of the forehead, between the eyebrows, and lastly to complete the symbolic cross and include the lowest psychic centre just below the navel.

Both the Baron and I had trouble with this, and Sufi Sahib had us fasting and refraining from sex, although to be honest there wasn't a lot of action at the Lodhi.

After a couple of days on the new regime my nafs, as the Sufi termed it, began to vibrate in unison and that evening Frederik's followed suit.

Sufi Sahib immediately changed the zikr to Ya Allah, which I must say was easier to do yet increased the intensity of the sensation into almost a pounding. For the final week with him we walked Delhi buzzing like bumblebees.

I feel I should add that Sufi Sahib refused all our efforts to compensate him. In fact we even had trouble giving him a jar of Orange Blossom honey we felt he might enjoy. Although Frederik eventually solved this dilemma by offering to provide him with a return trip to Mecca, which of course he was unable to resist.

For the Qalb zikr itself, its effects were subtle and far-reaching. I am not qualified to speak of the effect that attention brings to the inner psychic centres, but the difference between the wazifa, which is spoken, and the fikr, in which the mantra is cradled on the breath, can both become second nature, allowing thought to roam wherever it may. Yet in the case of the Qalb zikr, the portion of energy which thought uses for its meanderings are focussed on the speaking heart. Either it is or thought is, usually unnoticed thought, which some individuals term 'ego'.

And so it was some time later when I understood more fully the old dervish's farewell admonitions, that 'Power over others is distraction, power over oneself, presence'. For ultimately to be present in the present or maybe, present in the Presence, is about all we are required to be in this endless, timeless now that we are in.

Kneel before Zod, you bastards!

I am frequently asked by journalists and moviegoers alike what it was that gives General Zod, in the first few *Superman* movies (the director's cut of *Superman II*) such longevity. It is then the Nasruddin of Delhi springs to mind. Didn't Napoleon go east as a corporal and return a general?

Frederik continued on his journey to Japan. And I, on his recommendation, made my way to Bombay, and also on his direction checked in to the Taj Mahal Hotel, into the old section, with a view across Bombay Harbour; a recommendation I will always be grateful for.

This turn of events would become a pattern in our lives. He would catch up with me somewhere or I would get one of those delightful old telegrams with a name typed on a strip of white paper and stuck on the outside, invariably summoning me to some outlandish haven he'd discovered on his travels, or on even lengthier forays to help him convert his ancient Ibithiukan farm to be organic. The olive oil from his thousand-year-old trees was the finest I'd ever tasted. I also learned how to use it in short order cooking, in which the Baron excelled.

I digress. The whole of my initial venture and acceptance into India bore all the hallmarks of what these days I recognise as the Universe letting me know I was in the right place at the right time. The seeds were sown in the initial months I stayed in the Taj that would take and grow, allowing me to reinforce and understand Krishnaji's gracious guidance.

When I look back on the time between 1969 and 1977, I regard it as a retrograde period in my career, a slowing down when not much was happening. Yet only outwardly this was the case. There was acting work, but it was so far off the main thrust of showbiz I usually disregard it when contemplating the bulk of my performing work. One of these occasions was a job I returned to Europe for; a film entitled *A Season in Hell*, the saga of Arthur Rimbaud, to be shot in Rome for the Italian director Nelo Risi.

When I arrived at my chambers in Albany, the porter told me that a Baron and Baroness Van Pallandt had dropped by and left me a note. I rang right away and recognised Floris' voice, which I complimented him upon, to which he replied, 'I'm glad you reminded me. It's one of the things I felt might be of interest to you. Shall I drop by for tea? I'd like to see your set. D1 isn't it?' Which is how my renewed recourse into breath and consequently voice began, culminating in my appreciation that 'the voice is not only indicative of a man's character but it is the expression of his spirit'.

I had come upon a length of silk in India, which I'd bought intending to have it made into a shirt when I arrived in Rome. It was an unusual colour, what today might be described as an Yves-Klein blue. It was festooned over the back of one of the Bergere armchairs that a chum had needle-pointed for me. Of course Floris asked about it and I told him I felt it would make a cute shirt matched with a light grey suit.

'You should look for a gabardine. I've always thought gabardines have the most distinct greys.'

I could see where Frederik's taste came from.

After the event that changed Krishnamurti's life while in California, he continued to return periodically to India, in part to lecture and set up schools for children where they could study in a non-competitive environment. It was on one of these visits he was introduced to TKV Desikachar, reputedly the leading exponent of yoga. The two men appreciated each other, and this resulted in Krishnamurti starting to practice yoga.

Returning to Europe, he shared his new interest with his friend Contessa Vanda, who expressed a desire to study the ancient art. They decided to have Desikachar or one of his family join them at the annual retreat in Gstaad, Switzerland, to teach them both. Things proceeded splendidly (Vanda, it appeared, had a natural ability for all the asanas) until TKV sent across BKS Iyengar to lead the Swiss lectures and retreat. He repeatedly hurt Krishnamurti and the result was that he asked Vanda if she would continue his instruction.

'You never hurt me', he told her.

Some years later Mary Stewart, a London-based yoga teacher, took me to a teacher-pupil workshop given by Iyengar. Picking on me to show off his prowess, he had me reach forward with legs outstretched and touch my toes, whereupon he put his full body weight on my back and forced my face down onto my knees. I hobbled home but didn't get out of bed for days. When I pressed Krishnamurti for his opinion on Iyengar, he commented: 'He is … militant!'

My first shaved head role: *Kiss the Sky*

I would phrase it differently. He has one of the most pronounced egos I have ever come across in a professional yogi, a word signifying union, inwardly and outwardly. I only ever met him that one time and didn't stray from Vanda's teaching again until I knew what I was doing. Shooting *A Season in Hell* in Italy made it possible for me to have hands-on instruction from her. She never hurt me either. And it was my openness to her that not only allowed me to understand what a great teacher of yoga was, but also set up the physical path of diet and exercise that has kept me as flexible as I am these days.

While shooting *A Season in Hell*, with Jean-Claude Brialy portraying the fellow poet Verlaine, Nelo Risi, no doubt happy with my characterisation of the young genius and homosexual Rimbaud, came up with a follow-up project, the romantic tale of *Abelard and Heloise*, a spiritual couple who tasted another kind of forbidden love. As Nelo thought his best shot of getting the project financed would be to present the screenplay in English, he asked me to help him to find an English writer. I recommended my pal Frederik, who jetted into Rome to meet Nelo . They got on famously, and Frederik and I stayed on in Rome after *A Season in Hell* was completed.

It was a season in heaven for me. Rooming at the Inghilterra. Studying pranayama breath and yoga with Vanda. Discovering that vegetarianism was a lot more delicious than I had anticipated in the company of Frederik, who seemed to speak fluent Italian which, when I quizzed him on his gift, he modestly explained that being fluent in Spanish was a kick-start.

When the writing of *Abelard and Heloise* was complete, we both returned to the UK. It goes without saying that *A Season in Hell* turned out to be for four drag queens and Einstein, and *Abelard and Heloise* didn't even make it to the studio floor. It would be some years for me to portray a monk, not until *Kiss the Sky* came about later.

Back in London I received a telephone call from the headmistress of the newly set-up Krishnamurti school for children, Brockwood Park. I was invited to the ravishing bluebell-filled woods and fields of Hampshire for lunch. Apparently Krishnaji had expressed a notion that he support creative artists to visit the school when it was in session. I really hadn't expected him to be there in person, and was taken aback yet pleased to be sat opposite him at lunch again. Nothing much was said before lunch, yet he did ask me:

'Have you seen the señora?'

His face beamed such affection that I felt sure he was referring to Contessa Vanda.

'I have', I replied. 'She is very well. What a wonderful person she is.'
He smiled. 'She is.'

Encouraged by this friendly exchange, I feel I should explain that usually meetings between the sage and myself invariably began with a current discussion about the price of bespoke shoes – Lobbs, K, Cleverleys, me – new shirt makers, etc. And then a shift would occur. His tone of voice didn't exactly change, yet a shift was evident. I can only liken it to Cole Porter's lyric, 'How strange the change from major to minor'. As our current conversation had started in such an open way, I felt emboldened to ask him something that had been on my mind of some time.

'When your life changed that night, by the old pepper tree in Ojai, how would you describe what occurred?'

He considered the question before answering. Then he focussed his unblinking look into my eyes and said:

'The ocean fell into the drop.'

As it's been said before, it didn't improve the relationship but it ended that conversation.

Jeddu Krishnamurti

16

Adumbration, to forecast
a shadow. Or even two.

The first time I saw Marlon Brando on screen it completely changed how I felt about the actors I'd always admired. He opened a whole new dimension. There was no questioning his overwhelming masculinity, yet the feelings he evoked in his male viewers were as delicate as they were feminine. The most androgynous actor I'd previously come across, with a sense of comedy and timing equal to the best. Consequently my appreciation of James Dean and Montgomery Clift gave me a fresh understanding of the emotion I sometimes felt between 'Action' and 'Cut', which reinforced my belief that what I experienced watching these guys I could evoke, through the camera, in others. I began looking out for comedic roles to see if I could refine the comedy timing I'd felt at home with during my time on the boards.

The two teachers in my life were harmonizing really well for me. With Vanda I was learning yoga asanas to awaken the spine and the appropriate breath to enliven it. With Baron Floris I was privileged to share the esoteric secrets of the breath that Hazrat Inayat Khan had given to his closest of followers. During one such session Floris related a statement which might have been intended for the space between my own ears:

'It is the breath which connects the inner world with the outer world, just as the light thrown from the projector falls upon the cinema screen.'

Also:

'There is a certain degree of life in a person which can be distinguished by his breath, and that degree shows itself to the seer as colour and sound. Others can perceive it by a person's voice.

'Inspiration comes from the light thrown upon a certain idea. This comes from the radiance of the breath falling upon the mind. When the breath which is developed is thrown outward, its radiance produces light, and it is the different shades and grades of this light which manifest in various colours suggesting to the mystic the different elements which the particular colours denote. The same breath has a different action when it is thrown within. It falls upon the mind like a searchlight and shows to the intelligence the object of its search as things seen in daylight. Thus man knows without any effort on the part of the brain all he wishes to know, and expresses in the way each individual is qualified to express.

'There are two shadows, one that is projected upon the sky, another which falls upon the ground, the former known to the mystic and the latter to everyone.'

That is what the dervish in India implied by power over oneself. The shadow thrown upon the sky was the breath used by the individual when remembering himself, i.e. what was looking.

A tip received from both Vanda and Floris was to ensure that the tip of the tongue was on the roof of my mouth, just behind my upper teeth. With Vanda to remember to do it during my nostril breathing practices, with Floris during my practicing of fikar. I didn't ask why, and it wasn't until much later in life when I was being re-aligned by one of the UK's greatest chiropractors did he explain fully the significance.

Jon Howat practices just outside Oxford. It includes, when an appointment is available, a lengthy excursion on the Oxford Tube, a charabanc that runs between London and Oxford – yet it is more than worth it.

When I asked Jon if he knew anything of the tip of the tongue making contact with the roof of the mouth, he explained:

'The four pairs of mixed cranial nerves are generated embryologically on the 23rd day of one's formation – the trigeminal, the facial, the glossopharyngeal and the vagus. These mixed cranial nerves that are generated on the 23rd day are all inter-related and inter-dependent. Basically, the trigeminal runs the head, while the vagus runs the body. All the other sensory or motor cranial nerves do not generate until the 6th week. This is the survival kit that the baby, after birth, relies on.

'The mother's nipple goes into the baby's mouth and the lips and facial muscles latch on – this is the facial nerve. The tongue then presses the nipple against the roof of the mouth – the glossopharyngeal nerve. The sucking of the milk from the nipple comes from the trigeminal nerve. The swallowing of the milk, pumping of the heart, respiration, all the digestion, removal of nutrition from the milk and waste disposal, are all done by the vagus nerve.

'This integrated survival mechanism with the mother's nipple emphasises the cranial membrane structures, holds the brain in place and controls the brain circulation – blood in and blood out. This needs to be equal to bring about balanced intra-cranial pressure, enhanced brain and neurological physiology, and starts to reinforce the baby's natural ability to survive.'

Amazing what these early breath specialists worked out years ago.

Out of work in Ibiza

I knew it brought added awareness to my breath exercises yet didn't know the half of it. Yet it renewed my memories of a conversation I'd had, at the end of one of my early instruction sessions with Vanda. I had asked her how she had become involved with the practice of yoga, which she obviously appreciated. She explained that Krishnamurti, on returning from one of his many visits to the place of his birth, where he had set up several educational centres for children, had begun to notice that many of his contemporaries, the ones who appeared to be ageing gracefully in good health, invariably studied the ancient art of yoga and its complementary adjunct, pranayama, the complete practice of breath. He asked her, if he found a respected yoga teacher who would be prepared to come to Europe regularly to impart the knowledge, would it interest her to learn it with him. She was intrigued and delighted, and Krishnamurti set about locating the best exponent. She wasn't curious as to how it had come into being or why it worked so well. It just did, and that was sufficient for her. I followed her lead. However, during my lengthy sojourns in India, the discovery and provenance of the art aroused my own curiosity and I proceeded to find out for myself.

Most of the deep sources of yoga, and the mind-body wisdom they contain, differ dramatically from what is often taught as yoga in present day fitness outlets. Tirumalai Krishnamacharya (1888-1989) is considered that father of modern yoga. Most of the yoga one finds today at yoga studios taught here in the West comes via folks who studied with him, although he never left India. In his youth, and an early 'seeker', he heard of a sage who had left the busy stratum of city life and in his own voyage of self-discovery had retired to a cave in the Himalayas where he would be less distracted by the outside 'images' of the world and be able to come upon the 'aloneness' of pure wisdom, always present when the mind is at peace, yet fully aware. He located the man who was to teach him yoga; during the seven years he studied with him, it was only when he was advised to return to his everyday life that he made the promise to the guru he would carry on teaching the yoga he had discovered. He didn't have immediate impact and it was only when the Maharaja of Mysore took an interest in Kirshnamacharya and had him teach at his palace that his practice of emphasis on yoga for the individual was to become known as a requirement for the therapy of our age. His son TKV Desikachar maintained his lineage. And it was to Desikachar that Krishnamurti became a student.

When I moved into the set of chambers in St James, I marked the occasion by treating myself to a Roller, the last of the Silver Cloud model, which has never been topped for style in my book. It was Rolls Royce Velvet Green, almost black. In those days the West End wasn't gridlocked like it is today and there was parking space in the Albany forecourt. The car harmonised well with the great Routemaster buses, unlike the new so-called Routemasters with seats facing back-to-front designed to make travellers feel nauseous during rush hour, the only time they are used. Even the hop-on hop-off back doors designed to be reminiscent of the superb Routemasters are no longer staffed by TFL, which recycles all its profits to 'improve their service' – for whom, one wonders.

I received an unexpected telephone call from Dorothy Simmons, the headmistress of Brockwood Park School. Ravi Shankar was in town and wanted to play for Krishnamurti, would I be agreeable to pick up Ravi and his tabla player Chatur Lal and drive them to Brockwood? On the arranged day I drove to the address in Eaton Square to discover George Harrison leaving. Frederik always said George was the most accomplished guitarist of the Beatles.

'What are you up to, George?' I asked.

'Ravi is teaching me the sitar, it's a great instrument', he replied. He looked lit-up, inspired.

After George went on his way I was greeted warmly by Ravi and his tabla player, and their instruments were carefully loaded into the boot of the car.

The performance was given in the elegant circular room which I believe is now where the school meditates. I didn't know how much Krishnaji had been exposed to traditional Indian music, yet he seemed delighted to be sitting so close to it. A phrase I'd heard about from the great vina player Hazrat Inayat Khan came to mind: 'That among all the different arts, the art of music has been especially considered divine, because it is the exact miniature of the law working through the whole universe.'

In the early Seventies I was invited to go to Rome to meet Peppino Patroni-Griffi regarding a film he was about to make, provisionally entitled *The Divine Nymph*. It was to star an actress, unusually fetching, who was currently the most commercial star of the more risqué movies prevalent in Italy of the time. The role they wanted to meet me about was an Italian duke of the Thirties. I can't be sure if they wanted to see if Laura Antonelli wanted to work with yours truly, or more likely if they wanted to see if I could cut it as a local aristocrat. I decided I would go to see my folks in Plaistow to announce to them I would not be coming to lunch, as customary on Sunday. I never discussed my lack of employment with my parents, and whilst my Dad probably didn't concern himself, my Mum would have been aware of the state of play even though I had managed to keep up the money I gave them every month. So when I announced I wouldn't be at the weekly get-together as I was off to Rome, my mother interjected: 'Oh, have you got a job?'

'Well, it isn't an offer, it's only a "go see". They've given me an airplane ticket, albeit only economy! You never know, it sounds an interesting idea.'

Apparently after I left their house my Dad said: 'Listen, Ethel, get some money out of our bank account and make up the difference. He shouldn't be flying at the back of the bus.' I have to say, I didn't accept the cash, yet the offer of it made a deep impression on me. Apart from his terse comment about me being lucky after the *Billy Budd* premiere, it was the only other time he offered any insight into how he felt about his eldest boy's accomplishments. Yet, I guess if you ran away to sea aged fifteen and lied about your age to get aboard with a crew of older, hardened seafarers, the first thing you learn is to keep your trap shut.

I did get the job, and although the buxom Miss Antonelli was happily ensconced with her fella, there was enough snogging between 'Action' and 'Cut' for me to realise what a handful she would have been in any more intimate excursions. I also got to wear my first made-to-measure top hat, but can't recall if it made the final cut.

After I completed *The Divine Nymph*, retitled *The Divine Creature* for the English-speaking market, I landed another gig, *Striptease*, with another divine creature, Corinne Cleary. In spite of the title, I felt Corinne and I could make something of it and I believe it came out just fine.

17

Maharaj and Bhagwan

Fortified by good work and a few quid in the bank, I set out on another voyage to India. Great hotels keep a record of previous long-staying guests, and the Taj Mahal in Bombay was no exception. I was ushered into my old quarters overlooking the port.

Some of the families in the East have the tradition of giving their children names that have significant meanings. It is felt that the continual repetition of the word directed at the child will stimulate these innate qualities within them. When I discovered this tradition I frequently asked the meaning of people's names. One such person was a lovely receptionist in the old section of the hotel, named Neepa.

'Could I have a word with you, Mister Terence?'

'Of course. What does your name signify, Neepa?'

She smiled and hung her head. Through lowered eyes she said, 'Oh, it means light.'

'That's wonderful. I shall call you Radiance.'

As if to cover her embarrassment, she enquired, 'And what does your name mean?'

'Terence. I believe its original meaning was a seal or stamp, like with sealing wax.'

'So, you're a double stamp.'

'You could say. And the word you wanted with the hefty stamp?'

'This really is none of my business, but I've noticed visitors who ask for you are of the Muslim persuasion, they seem rather serious folk.'

'They are, yes. I'm not only on vacation in India. I'm interested in the deeper understanding of life that's practiced here in the East.'

'Are your enquiries directed to any particular faith?'

'On the contrary. Wisdom doesn't have favourites, as I understand it can arise anywhere.'

'Yes.'

This affirmation ushered in a rather long, not uncomfortable pause, then: 'A friend of mine has heard about a gentleman, he is from the Hindu tradition but...'

'You can speak openly with me, Radiant one, it stays between you and me.'

'It's only that he is extremely low caste. He sold beedis. He resides in the poor quarter of Bombay, Khetwadi. It's a little squalid.'

'What's a beedi?'

'Oh, it's an Indian cigarette, that's how he made his living before... before...'

'He became special.'

'Yes. He only speaks Murati, but I believe has good translators when he talks and answers questions. I don't have a precise address, yet most folks in Khetwadi know where he is. His name is Sri Nisargadatta Maharaj."

Which is how the Jnani, or wise one, known as Maharaj, came into my life.

On my first visit to Khetwadi, the phrase 'everyone is born an eagle, how high you fly is your choice' came to mind. I realised how appropriate the eagle reference was when I climbed the ladder to go through the hole in the ceiling which became the hole in the floor which the daughter of Maharaj had incorporated halfway across her living room to give her father a space of his own.

The eyes that locked into mine as my head appeared into his space were eagle-like indeed. On leaving the Taj, the doorman, who had summoned the taxi, asked me my destination. When I commented 'Khetwadi', he gave me what my gran would have called an old-fashioned look. Seeing my blank expression, he added, without judgement, 'It is the cat district, Sahib.' He didn't mean our four-legged friends.

Maharaj, as I came to know him, resided in a small, old apartment block, in front of which was an open sewer. Before negotiating the best way to ford this waterway bubbling with refuse, I saw opposite a public latrine. As I had no idea of what would await me inside or how long the audience would take, I decided to relieve myself before I found out. Maharaj had no telephone and I had no appointment. The stench when I entered the public lavatory was like no other I had encountered. Further investigation revealed why. The stalls were a cornucopia, filled to overflowing with stools of all shapes and sizes, and the stand-up urinals battlements of a similar order. Ramparts of shit piled chest-high. In spite of the overwhelming abasement of my olfactory organs, my curiosity was aroused. How had it been achieved? The customers must have been gymnasts, leaping somersaults to relieve themselves!

I stepped over the creek of sewage and entered the humblest of dwellings, my bladder unrelieved. Once through the opened front door, the ladder angled up into a square, cut into the ceiling. On the floor at its base, several pairs of shoes. I was joined by a young woman, his daughter, who motioned me to climb. As my head went through the opening I had a moment to see the living space that had been created by utilising the high ceiling of the original room, before a newspaper was lowered by one of the group and my eyes were gripped by the most penetrating gaze I have encountered. As I clambered up into the room, in which I couldn't straighten up, I looked around. The very thin man with the piercing eyes said something in a language I couldn't follow and motioned me to sit down. I did. Both of the older men, who had been absorbed in sections of the Times of India, also lowered their news sheets, and one of them said in accented English: 'Maharj says to make yourself comfortable and meditate.'

I felt the coconut matting through my khadi drawstring pyjama trousers. The air in the room was filled with the smoke from burning joss sticks. It was that inexpensive, sweet kind, and strong – obviously – to offset the latrine opposite and the sewer below. My mind wasn't steady at all, but I reassured myself with the fact that at least I had made it. Maharaj had returned to his broadsheet. It transpired that the guru didn't speak any English and was awaiting a translator, who appeared through the floor a few minutes later. Then the inquisition began.

'Who are you?' was his first question.

'I am Terence, from England.'

'Yes. But who are you?'

'I am an actor.'

'Yes, but who is an actor?'

'I – I'm me.' I started to feel like an idiot.

'Who is me?'

I could only gesture. Helpless.

He continued to stare at me, like a bird of prey eyeing a mouse. Finally he spoke. The translator translated, 'Come back tomorrow. 11am.'

The satsang is terminated. He fires up a beedi, the local cigarette, aforementioned; a dry leaf rolled around a few strands of tobacco.

I touched my forehead. I feel like a serf. I thank the translator, who speaks perfect English, without an accent. 'You speak better English than me.'

'Thank you. I'm frequently told that. See you tomorrow.'

I left the building, stepped over the sewer, and turned left. I got to the end of the road and saw a cafe. I went in and ordered some chai. I needed it. I felt I had been let out of school at the end of a long, tough first day. The tea arrived in a china cup with a saucer. It was very sweet, a blast from the past. It reminded me of a taste from the Blitz. I later discovered they make it with condensed milk.

The axiomatic questioning continued on the second visit. Until finally I owned up. I don't know who or what I am. Not really

This momentarily satisfied him. His attention focused on the other listeners sitting cross-legged around the space.

One of the group – he was a Canadian and a newcomer like myself – asked, or rather stated: 'I've heard you are a Jnani (master) and yet you are a chain smoker.'

'Who's a chain smoker?' the translator relayed. As the dialectic of Mahara consisted initially of bringing to our attention that we are not our bodies or our minds, it was a given that he had long since severed any identification with his. Ironically this felt like the wall that I ran into with Krishnamurti: I understood the words, yet no insight, the very reason I had returned East to find a ladder I could approach a few rungs down.

'How are you finding Master Maharaj?' Neep enquired as I passed her to go to my room

'Well, I found him. That was a start!'

'My brother said he's austere. If that's the right word.'

'Yeah. I haven't come across anyone quite as heavy. I guess I'm a bit dense! I've been thinking about taking a break, let it all settle, maybe check in again later.'

'Sounds like a good idea. I'm happy you feel he is worth it.'

'Oh, no question. It's me. I came to India to loosen up a bit.'

Later that day just outside the Taj a group of brightly dressed young men were having a discussion. They saw me observing them and called me over. They sounded like Americans. I indicated their bright orange outfits.

'What's this then?' I asked.

'We're with Rajneesh. We're sannyasins.'

On closer examination they all had wooden bead necklets, malas round their necks with a man's picture.

'You've never heard him. Bhagwan?'

'Bhagwan?'

'Bhagwan Rajneesh. What do you do?'

'I'm an actor, just looking around.'

'An actor.'

Another in the group joined in.

'An actor, you should definitely check him out. He's coming from a special place, yet the way he puts across his ideas, he's the most impressive speaker I've ever heard.'

'Is he in town now?'

'No, his ashram is in Poona. It is a train ride. Well worth the trip. Check him out. Tell them on the gate Swami Yoga-yogi sent you.'

'Swami Yogi, is that you?'

'Yeah, everyone who is initiated gets a new name.'

A few days later I found myself arriving in the charming town of Poona and checking into the Blue Diamond Hotel, recommended to me at the train station.

The Blue Diamond was a typical Indian hotel, not much different from Western hotels save the fact that the bathroom was an empty enclosed space with a bucket, water tap and a hole in the middle of the room toward which all the floor sloped.

The concierges were as good as anywhere; they were also filmgoers, albeit of local fare known to us as Bollywood movies. The room I had been assigned was neat and spotless. I came upon a few postcards advertising the establishment. I addressed one to the long-suffering Jimmy Fraser at his office in Regent Street, letting him know I was OK.

That evening I did a recce of the ashram. From the outside it looked like a medley of local houses enclosed by hastily assembled wall surround. I enjoyed a tasty vegetarian curry which came with brown rice. It was the first inkling of how much the well-heeled seekers who wend their way to the ashram were exerting influence on local businesses.

When I presented myself at the common entrance the next morning I didn't need any recommendations, as I was welcomed with open arms and a darshan was arranged for later that day. The place was a hive of engaged activity. Sannyasins, as everyone was known, were of all ages, yet mostly youths of both sexes. All clad in every line of orange. Most had long hair, the males were mostly unshaven or bearded. All attractive in their own way and from all corners of the world.

I soon discovered that Bhagwan Shri Rajneesh had been a star professor and lecturer at a prominent Indian university prior to discovering his true calling, and adopting, or giving himself, his present title. There was no mention of the guru who engineered or guided his life, or how he came to be so well set-up. His personal companion, who shared his quarters, was described as pale as an English rose and in her early twenties. I confess I was curious to come face-to-face with the great man who I'd heard from all was unlike all the sages I had studied, with the exception of George Gurdjieff, who had left Russia and brought some of his devotees with him, including his niece Elaine, who'd married one

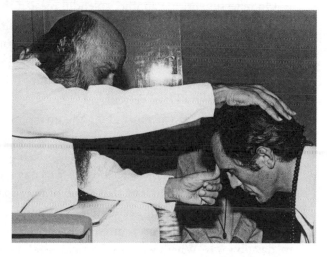

Bhagwan Shri Rajneesh and splendid hands

of the initial students of Gurdjieff on his arrival in Paris. Russell Page, the distinguished landscape gardener, I had met and discussed with at length the Russian's unorthodox antics in his efforts to reveal the light.

Prior to my own introduction to the Bhagwan, it had been made clear to me that if he offered to initiate me I should accept, as it was considered a big honour.

My name was called and I walked forward and sat in front of the man. He wasn't what you would call handsome. His rotund stature resembling more Charles Laughton than Orson Welles, until he spoke; that was when he became the sum of the two, along with Albert Finney and Oliver Reed, to name a few. I haven't spoken of his hands. They were unusually fine, delicate yet not without strength. His voice plus these appendages would have most women halfway there.

I was offered initiation, which I accepted. And was given a new name and a wooden mala complete with Bhagwan's image, which he dropped over my head and then pressed my forehead with his exquisite thumb. I assumed he was opening my third eye. I have to confess there was no instant effect from the pressured chakha. My new name, Swami Deva Veeten, meant Master of the Divine Beyond. I was also welcomed to take up residence inside the ashram. This meant I would live for free, as all meals were provided. I could move in the next day.

On reflection during another splendid meal at the Blue Diamond, I considered my encounter with the Bhagwan. He differed initially from Maharaj in that whilst he considered most folks completely identified with their concept of themselves, he not only advised them to observe and let go of it, he gave them a brand new one complete with a meaningful name. Ergo, Swami Deva Veeten!

At the first meal as a member of the ashram it came to my notice that all the swamis and the 'mas' who were dining alone were busying themselves as well as eating. Some had books, or were correcting manuscripts, others just reading ingredients on sauce bottles. I recognised this as something I often did myself: Could it be that either pre-occupation was enhanced by the dual awareness, or divided? The phrase I'd heard Mararaj use to admonish a seeker who wanted to know the best specific time for medication was 'What's wrong with right now!' I chewed my breakfast thinking about the others around me and then focused my attention on the actual taste in my mouth. Of course it was different, tastier. Was there a secret in the mind's ability to consider two things at the same time, or was it as Maharaj had pointed out, 'People keep busy because they find it difficult to bear their own consciousness.'

Bhagwan's morning lectures were a delight. He rarely expounded on subjects that hadn't been committed to print before, and every word was recorded and duly produced in book form. Hence the dozens of his books available. Yet for me it was as my original sannyasin had predicted for anyone interested in public speaking; to listen to him in the flesh was a unique, special event. During the early morning sessions I was enthralled by his delivery, timing and seeming freedom with the comic opportunities embraced us all. Embedded in my own psyche was the way he gathered the energy of his audience between his outstretched arms, complimented, as it were, by those fine yet strong hands.

It is intriguing that it is these aspects of Rajneesh I took back with me on my return to showbiz, and how they became the bridge I negotiated from youthful leading man to middle-aged character actor without the need to sacrifice anything.

On some Sunday mornings a group of British sannyasins, newly converted from Curzon and Lyall to Indian venerables, would get together at the Blue Diamond Hotel for what we thought of laughingly as Full English Breakfast. Anything considered remotely English or British – fried egg, beans on toast, welsh rabbit, muffins, crumpets – was served up, usually on a single large plate. On the morning in question, as we were moving from the front door to the restaurant, the concierge hailed me.

'Oh, Mr Terence, we have a cable for you, sir.'

He rummaged behind his front counter, producing the famous yellow telegram, a little dusty and dog-eared, I must say. God knows how long it had been there. He placed it reverentially in my opened hand. As I took in the white name and address strips fastened to it, it seemed as if its psychic weight increased. Clarence Stamp. The Rough Diamond Hotel. Poona, India. Even as I slit it open I knew my life was about to change:

COULD YOU RETURN TO LONDON FOR
SUPERMAN 1 AND 2 TO BE DIRECTED BY RICHARD DONNER.
YOUR PART WOULD BE GENERAL ZOD.
YOU HAVE SCENES WITH MARLON BRANDO.

I gave the concierge a generous tip. (All tips in rupees seem generous.) 'Could you book me a call to London, this afternoon, say about 4 o'clock.' Five hours behind us, Jimmy Fraser should be at his desk. 'The number is Regent 7311.'

Fraser's reassuring Scottish voice told me the part was mine if I agreed. He had shown the casting director some footage of my duke from *Divine Creature*. Yes, Marlon was set to play *Superman*'s father, and an unknown named Christopher Reeve was set for the hero. I would be the Kryptonite villain. A 'yes' would do for now. 'Yes, if you're back in a couple of weeks you could meet up with the director then', Fraser told me.

I set up an interview with Bhagwan to discuss the new situation.

'You've spent your time well, Veeten, go with my blessings.'

I caught the midday train to Bombay, it being my intention to attend a few morning sessions with Maharaj before getting the plane back to Blighty.

It may have been my imagination, yet I felt warmly received back in the converted garret in Khetwadi. Although on leaving that first morning another disciple had told me in hushed tones that Maharaj had been diagnosed with throat cancer and no one knew how long he had for this world.

The very next morning a newcomer, a youngish Canadian, commented: 'You are considered a great jnana and I've heard have a serious throat condition, why is it you are still smoking?'

'Who has a serious throat condition?' was his reply.

At the end of the meeting I drew Mr Sapre and his wife aside and asked if there was anything I could do for Maharaj.

Mr Sapre said he wanted for nothing, but Mrs Sapre assured me he would love to be invited to the Taj for tea.

The old section of the Taj Mahal Hotel has been kept in the spirit in which it was designed. But there is a rumour quite in keeping with the continent's whimsical reputation. The hotel was designed and constructed to commemorate Queen Victoria's visit to the jewel in the crown of the Empire. The architect awarded the design came to Bombay, selected the site, and chose the finest of the country's materials. He appointed a Master Builder to oversee the project and sailed home to Britain. On notification that the project had been completed, he booked passage to India, intending to sail into the Bay of Bombay and see his masterwork from the ship, as his sovereign would see it on her arrival. As the liner neared the port, with the architect standing proudly on the prow of the ship, he realised something was amiss. The Master Builder and his crew, left to their own devices, had built the hotel back to front. The architect killed himself. It doesn't do to take your eye off the ball in the construction business, in India or anywhere else.

The natives have idiosyncratic ways of making the best of a bad job. A swimming pool was designed to fit into the circular design of the front, now the back, and the rooms designed to face onto the city, which now faced the sea, were upgraded.

Sri Nisagadatta Maharaj

It was pleasing to do something for the Maharaj, the man who appeared to have nothing yet was everything. It was in the first floor restaurant, named the Sea Lounge, that I met Maharaj for tea. He arrived with Mr and Mrs Sapre. His usually crumpled khadi kurta and pyjamas were crisp and lightly starched, and he was sporting a sparkly-red short-sleeved woolly pullover, which perfectly complimented his birth sign, Sagittarius. As he stomped up the wide, carpeted stairs toward the entrance to the Sea Lounge, grasping his long walking stick, he looked like any other Bombay walla of a certain age who hadn't bought into western gear and persisted with the traditional white khadi so perfect for the climate. Ascending the stairs, he didn't even raise a glance from passers-by, and I wondered how often in my own life I had passed an individual who had been blessed – that Krishnamurti had described as 'the ocean fell into the drop'. Or as the fella I was taking to tea, who in answer to the enquiry about his own condition had stated, 'The Universe floats within me as a cloud in the sky.'

Settled around a window table with a view of the ocean was arranged quite a high tea, with a large pot of Assam's best small leaf tea, a jug of hot water, and tea strainers. No tea bags at the Taj.

A fellow tourist, an American, who was also staying at the hotel, decided he would crash the party. He was by profession a 'channeler', giving health tips and emotional help from an 'old Chinese guide' on the other side. He didn't actually take a chair, but semi-sat on the broad sill in the window and listened to what Maharaj, via Mr Sapre, was saying.

Then he asked: 'Look, I am married. A very nice woman, we have two kids. She's not dumb, but she doesn't understand things the way I do. It's awkward socially. Any advice?'

Maharaj didn't pause. 'Who is this "I" you refer to? Show him to me. If you can't, then wake up from the dream and ask where are the others.'

He left without so much as sipping his cup of Assam. Mr Sapre told me that Maharaj gave short shrift to seekers 'who want to wake up while remaining comfortably asleep'.

While we enjoyed our tea Mrs Sapre asked me how I came to him. I told him I had heard of him from someone at the Taj, whose brother had listened to him. Mrs Sapre re-posed the question: 'How did you find this path?'

'I was in my twenties making a film in Rome for Federico Fellini.

I was invited to a lunch with Krishnamurti.' Maharaj interjected: 'Krishnamurti?' I asked Mr Sapre: 'Does Maharaj know Krishnamurti?'

'He hasn't met him. Yet he knows of him.'

'What does he feel about Krishnamurti?'

After a moment, Maharaj stated: 'We are in the same ancient condition.'

At the end of our tea, knowing it would be unlikely I would ever see the great man again, and wanting to prolong the moment, I strolled with them to the front of the Taj. As I shook hands with Maharaj he looked into my eyes and said:

'Your nature is already perfect. Pay attention to "that" which is always with you. You must feel its necessity!'

18

Kneel before Zod!

The first call I made upon my return from Bombay was to my chum Herbert Kretzmer. The *Superman* scripts had been awaiting me at Albany and I needed his advice. He'd just moved into a new flat in Basil Street and invited me to meet him there, a hundred yards from the Fire Station.

'Of course you should do it. You haven't been in big films for years. What's the problem?'

'I know it's all good. I just don't feel confident. The part is OK, the villain. I'm not sure I can pull it off.'

'Terence. It's one thing to be modest, it's another not to have confidence in oneself.'

It struck me as ironic that Herbie should be advising me in this fashion, as he was the most modest, unassuming man I've ever come across. He continued, 'Besides, you can use the cash, right?'

I have usually valued Herbie's advice and, reassured by him, I went off to meet Richard Donner. The first thing that struck me about the director was that he had a genuine sense of fun, needed to bring life into the great comic character of the Fifties. He didn't bring up any of my stuff that he'd seen and you never actually knew whether the footage one's agent has made available is seen by the director or if they just accept the casting director's recommendation. He appeared keen to have me on board. So I accepted.

Costume and make-up tests followed, and it soon became apparent the DP was under instructions to make me look as dodgy as possible. I guessed my days as a leading man were over. I voiced my concerns to Frederik, who had left his family in Chelsea and secured chambers above mine in Albany, D6, which was on the top floor.

'Don't concern yourself. This film has got your name on it and, believe me, if they can make it look like a man can fly, every kid in the world will want to see it. And, in my view, most kids today are going to relate to the super-villain than to the guy who wears his underpants over his trousers.'

The Baron was usually right in his predictions and it was the first time anyone had referred to General Zod as the super-villain. He also suggested I listen to the classical piece 'Zadok the Priest' to get me in the mood.

One of the special blessings in my life which came to pass once I had left home and became an actor was that life brought me into contact with heavy people.

As I had been away from London for some time, I decided to look up some of my old chums. I was looking for some sheet music in South Kensington and had the impulse to check out Lionel Bart. But when I entered Reece Mews a figure I knew was coming from the other end. It was Francis Bacon, who I had met with Geoffrey Bennison some time before, in the Sixties, as I recalled. I wasn't sure if he would remember me but I said hello anyway. He did, and explained that Lionel no longer resided next door. He told me that Lionel had moved to a bigger house, nearer Fulham. He had his new address somewhere, and invited me in.

His studio was a tip. Taking in my obvious reaction to the chaos, he explained he preferred to create in this atmosphere. It crossed my mind that Beethoven liked to create in similar chaos. I wouldn't have thought that Beethoven exuded this comfortable melancholy as Francis did. I kind of understood this as, though for the most part I looked upon myself as a neat freak, there were times when I just let everything slide. If I was about to play a character who was elegant, a few weeks before the work was to start I would wear the same gear day after day, not even bothering to change my t-shirt.

As Francis had opened the subject to his creative process, I explained a bit about my own feelings with regard to film acting. We had much in common, the main thing was our understanding of the moment and our efforts to feel it unadorned, not fragmented by thought. I don't know if I was particularly open, resonating with Maharaj's recent guidance to wake up and be aware, yet I felt at ease. Francis seemed equally comfortable and we shared our experience of feeling a thrill or kind of joy doing the creation, and the melancholy that followed when we realised the sense of 'otherness' was not our own even though we felt it inside ourselves.

The closeness we shared ended as abruptly as it had come about. I felt he had something pressing to do. I excused myself. On my way out I glimpsed a startling portrait on an easel – deep, foreboding, yet startling. I thought, my God, if I could evoke that depth to General Zod he would be a super-villain.

It never rains, it pours, the saying goes. A frantic summons from agent James Fraser: Peter Brook is making a film of George Gurdjieff's book *Meetings with Remarkable Men*. He is interested in me to play Prince Lubovedsky, one of Gurdjieff's early influences. Peter Brook is one of the world's leading theatre directors. He is credited with some of the finest theatre productions of the modern era. This would be one of his few films. Gurdjieff's book is only the second he ever penned. It features the remarkable people he met on his spiritual journey.

I had read *Remarkable Men* on Russell Page's recommendation. It all sounded good, including a location in Afghanistan. The problem arose when Fraser explained I would be used during the *Superman* schedule. Out of work all this time, now conflicting schedules! That's showbiz for ya.

I asked Jimmy what he thought. He voiced two facts: Richard Donner had sounded enthusiastic about me, and they were asking for a long shooting commitment during which I would actually only work intermittently. He would get the dates when Peter Brook needed me on set, and perhaps I could shoot both. How did I feel about that – was I up for it? Was time showing me its own movie? I felt brimming with energy.

I used the moment before completely engaging with work to make a trip to Brockwood to vibe myself up, so to speak.

The woman who had created the estate at Brockwood long before it was taken over by the Krishnamurti Foundation had imported soil from California, from the area where the giant Redwoods grow, to enable the Redwood saplings to flourish in England. The plan had worked and the trees were now giants like their ancestors in the US. They were an essential part of the Grove, the section of the grounds where Krishnaji so liked to be.

What I hadn't expected on this unannounced visit was for himself to be in residence, and when I came upon him he seemed less welcoming than usual. He said rather tersely: 'You don't find this in a supermarket.'

I was more than taken aback, lost for words, in fact. And he moved on.

I came to the conclusion that he must have heard of my excursion to

Poona and the goings on in orange. Taking stock on the train back to Waterloo it came to me how much meeting him had meant to me and how his continued interest in my development had altered the course of my life. As the train rattled along, stopping at some stations and passing others, I saw my life not in the triumphs and failures of my movie career, but from a different standpoint: before and after my fateful meeting with this great sage. I knew how I felt about him. What was hard for me to embrace was just how much care he had brought from his side. All I could do now, for the moment, from this moment, was to be more mindful.

James Fraser successfully negotiated for the two films to dovetail. I would shoot *Remarkable Men* during the gaps of schedule on the *Superman* films, the two weeks on location in Afghanistan with Peter Brook slotting neatly into a three-week break with Richard Donner. It was akin to my days in weekly repertory theatre, when we would open in a new play on Monday night and only barely remembering the lines we would begin rehearsing for next week's production first thing on Tuesday morning. In truth I was excited and hyped up by the possibility.

My first face-to-face with Brando completely lived up to my expectations. He was traveling with not one but two girls, both sultry-skinned, and I gathered, sisters – what else? As I came on set he saw me, and after a moment with them came over to introduce himself.

'Hi, I'm Marlon Brando.'

I knew very well that he was Marlon Brando, and what's more he knew very well that I knew he was Marlon Brando.

It was the ironic humour I'd heard so much about, in person.

I grasped his outstretched hand.

'It is a great pleasure to meet you, Marlon Brando.'

He immediately drew me close to him.

'See those two girls over there?'

They were giggling together.

'Yeah.'

'They want your dick.'

'What about your dick, Marlon?'

'They've had my dick. Now they're interested in yours.'

Could we say we got off on the right dick!

A lot of the shooting was tough on the body, which entailed not only *Superman*, but the other Kryptonites flying. Very sophisticated yet painful nevertheless. My scenes with Marlon, however, were a delight, and enlightening. The first set-up we did together, the camera was only on him, I was his eye-line, off camera. Initially it didn't appear he was taking it seriously, yet on 'Action' when I burst into life he became equally galvanised. During the break, while we waited for the cameras to be repositioned, I asked him about the rumours that he no longer took his performing seriously, unlike his great earlier work.

He pondered for a moment and then said in that wonderfully, quite high voice that could explode into volumes of fury: 'I began to notice that sometimes when I invested myself in a take, the director would automatically call for another.'

'I know the feeling.' It was one of the great drawbacks of working with film-makers who had only mastered the technical aspects of filmmaking.

He continued: 'For a laugh I decided, as they weren't interested in the feelings I was having, I would not bother. That's how it began. You're the first person to ask me about it. Donner holds me to a line, but most don't even notice.'

I'd heard that he was being paid a million dollars for twelve days' work, so when he showed up for work on what was his thirteenth day, I enquired:

'I thought your deal was for twelve days, isn't this day 13?'

He grinned.

'Today is gratis.' The grin widened.

After Marlon completed his work, the technical difficulties involved with the stunts, mainly the aerial stuff, became manifest, which apparently slowed down the production. When I returned after my *Meetings* location, there were rumours that Richard Lester, known mainly for his filming with the Beatles, had been seen around the studio. And Dick Donner, who as I said before was shooting *Superman I* and *II* simultaneously, had been told to 'just complete *Superman I*'.

Which he consequently did. Upon completion he was fired and replaced by Richard Lester. It's hard to comprehend a director of the stature of Lester going along with this: he must have known from the assemblage of Donner's footage it was his masterwork. Yet hey! It's showbiz, right?

There was more to come. When we all returned to work after the hiatus during which Donner's first part had opened to groundbreaking reviews and world-record box office takings, we discovered that all of Brando's footage as *Superman*'s father was being cut. His character was being re-shot as *Superman*'s mother, played by the English actress Susannah York. It took a little digging to discover the reason to re-do perfectly good footage with the greatest actor of the modern era with a beautiful yet little-known performer. When the film began its huge success at the box office, Brando's representative exercised their contractual rights and requested Marlon's percentage points. In anticipation of the even bigger gross by *Superman*, the producers Pierre Spengler and Ilya Salkind had cut Marlon from the second instalment to weaken his case in the event of a lawsuit.

It took Richard Donner twenty years to retrieve his original footage and, with Warner Bros' blessing, to assemble and re-release *Superman II – The Director's Cut*. Well worth a look, folks!

19

Seduced by glamour

The initial meeting with the distinguished theatre director Peter Brook was at his house in Holland Street, Kensington. I met Dragon Maksimovic, the Yugoslav actor cast to play the young Gurdjieff. Also Jeanne de Salzmann, now in her eighties. She had left Russia with Gurdjieff when he fled to France to avoid the Russian Revolution. Whilst born in Geneva in 1889, she trained as a dancer and was teaching eurhythmics when she met Gurdjieff in Tiflis, Georgia, in 1919. When she and her husband settled in Fontainebleau she became an integral part of its Institute for the Harmonious Development of Man, where she and her pupils gave the first performances of Gurdjieff's 'sacred dances' that were to be the climax of the *Meetings with Remarkable Men*, which she would co-direct with Brook.

During the Holland Street get-together, it was made clear to the actors the 'degree of presence' which Brook and de Salzmann would expect of us.

If one cuts through the extraordinary and humorous devices of Gurdjieff's teaching, the fundamental premise isn't different from Krishnamurti or Maharaj. What is unique are the sacred dances, which embody in movement the 'self-remembering' he encouraged in his instruction.

One of the current tests for Parkinson's Disease that doctors give potential sufferers is to hold their hands in front of them as still as possible while the practitioner gives them simple mathematical equations to solve. For example, 'What is 6 plus 3?', yet gradually increasing in complexity, so: 6 plus 3, add 11, now subtract 7, etc. At a certain point when the brain is more actively engaged, the attention to keeping the hands still is directed to the problem and they begin to shake. When you first see the sacred dances you understand just how great the increase in awareness is called upon to perform them.

It was exhilarating to be in the wide openness of Afghanistan and away from Pinewood Studios. Mme de Salzmann proved a joy to work with and be with. She slotted in effortlessly not only with Peter Brook but all the cast and crew, striding across the hills en route to the location, often the first to arrive and invariably the last to leave. I began to appreciate Joanna Lumley's long held wish to 'be older', with its wisdom and understanding. One conversation with Jeanne springs to mind:

'When Mr G spoke of "self-remembering" how did he mean it to be interpreted?' I asked.

'It is the opposite of self-forgetfulness. When the attention is so taken up with the surroundings, that which is outside oneself, what he sometimes called "the glamour", oneself is forgotten. Equally so when the movement of awareness, caused by thought, distracts from what is seeing the "I Am".'

'So self-remembering is when the movement of thought is included in what is being seen and awareness of what is actually looking, which is always unmoving?'

'That's correct.'

'So, present in the present.'

'Yes. What we are hoping to illustrate in the film making.'

It was a great experience I had in Afghanistan, beautiful—even more so the people.

It was during the combined combo of the *Superman* and *Meetings* films that I became aware of the endless yet appropriate newness inside the stillness that occurred with the ending of thought—what Krishnamurti later termed 'the movement of the alone, only then the never-ending journey of the unknowable'.

It was endlessly reassuring to me that I was able to bestride the blackness of Zod and the light of Lubodevsky.

If it was exhilarating to leave Pinewood it was equally so to return, bringing with me my first experience of practicing the level of awareness, usually my private pre-occupation, shared with directors and cast. On the days when I was working on the *Superman* sets I would visit the *Meetings* set in the lunch break , in my General Zod outfit, and suck up the vibes from the *Remarkable Men* stage.

By the time both epics were complete, I had reassured myself the transition to embrace character performer and leading man was accomplished.

20

Die before death

When *Superman II* was released its commercial success did bring some interesting work my way, such as *The Vatican Conspiracy* in which I played a Pope. My Mum was pleased, but also my agent was contacted by the producer Jeremy Thomas.

The Hit was an original, scripted by Peter Prince. I thought it was great, a thriller in a dark comedy vein, so I met with the director Stephen Frears at my apartment. We got along fine. I later heard he'd been impressed with my book-lined walls. Similar to the ones he'd envisaged for the character he was about to cast.

The Hit was basically a road movie revolving around three men: the hit man, his apprentice, and the victim. Joe Strummer, the head man from The Clash, had been set for Myron, the apprentice, but he bottled out at the last minute and was replaced with Tim Roth, who'd done a bit of British television and a lot on the boards of the Glasgow Citizens' Repertory. His transformation to film was seamless.

John Hurt signed to play Braddock, the hit man. I couldn't have been more pleased, as I had admired him from afar for years. A consummate pro, he appeared to have no problems with any of the three mediums – stage, TV or film.

The whole shoot was on location, the length and breadth of Spain. One of the themes woven into the text is death. My character Willie has betrayed a big gang boss in London in exchange for his freedom and a new identity, and has lived for many years preparing for his inevitable assassination.

The hit man's assignment is to locate him and deliver him to the man he betrayed, who intends to execute him personally.

There is a key sequence where Willie tries to convince Braddock, his captor (John Hurt), that death is only the price of having had an individuality. In other words, he accepts his fate. To this end, Willie reads

Braddock a John Donne sonnet.

A great sonnet is a test for any actor, and John Donne's are considered to be amongst the finest. The first hurdle is that, ideally, the sonnet should be read while sustaining the intent of the piece. I had tried to recite the fourteen lines in a single breath but failed. In the screenplay, Willie reads the sonnet, which he carries with him. True to my game plan of 'learning the wordies' in every scenario, I committed the scene and the poem to memory.

As it was the pivotal scene between Mr Hurt and myself, I spent much time working on it in order to be as open as possible on the night, and put in many hours the night before.

Murphy's Law, or Sod's Law as we Londoners call it, prevailed. Bad weather caused the shooting of the sequence to be postponed not once but twice, and only on the third try was it actually committed to film.

The other thing I should mention is that whilst a lot of directors and actors are usually happy to get it on the first take, others use the first take as a rehearsal on film. It worked against me on this shoot, as both John and Stephen are in the latter category.

On the master shot, John and I played the complete scene. It went well, and the camera was being reset for the singles when I felt a delicate shift in consciousness and knew from past experience there was not actually anything I could do to prolong or strengthen this shift – this was going to be the moment.

I stayed quiet. Relaxed on my mark as the minimal changes to the light plan were carried out. We were ready. Everyone was in place.

'Stand by. Camera. Action.'

In that moment, I settled into the stillness which encompasses everything, and the words seemed to flow effortlessly from it.

Then, suddenly, there were strident voices in the distance; shouts cracking the calm.

The sound man called 'Cut!'

An assistant was dispatched to quiet the noise makers.

Thoughts that were only background shadows became front and centre in my mind. Willie was gone. Terence was back. The moment passed.

That feeling of utter loss was beginning ...

Silence.

I take a deep breath. I wait. I feel the energy of our focused crew. I offer myself to it. My thoughts slow, becoming once more static on the surface of an awareness that extends in all directions. The dialogue wells up once more. Is spoken.

An unfamiliar sensation – condition would be a more apt description – as if every word that comes out of my mouth is accommodated by a prepared space; airy fingers into a delicate made-to-measure doeskin glove.

The take ends. The camera stops. The soft, pervasive space becomes, once again, the canvas on which the less subtle ambience arises.

I feel no impulse to do or say anything. Yet a few of the burly technicians come close to me. One grins. One rubs my shoulder. Camera is repositioned on John. We do his single. The first take is good.

Stephen asks if he'd like another. John gives one of his lugubrious grins. 'I don't think anyone will be watching me when Terence is in this mood', he concludes, including me in his eye line.

21

I always loved my mother to excess

My mother died when I was in the middle of *Legal Eagles* in New York. The grief will be familiar to anyone who has lost a parent. I was not able to get back to London for the funeral so I bade my farewell by way of a letter I wrote to her. In a gesture I felt she might appreciate, I set fire to it in Central Park, opposite the New York Athletic Club where I was billeted. Even as the coil of ash fell to the ground, I felt a measure of peace; but, very soon, on the walk back across Central Park South, the memories returned, bringing the sadness with them as I relived our life together.

Into this conceptual overlay came a few dominant words, 'write it down', which were repeated at intervals until I reached my monastic lodgings on the twentieth floor. I found my pen, but the only paper available was the blank side of my script for the film I was working on. I turned it over and, opening it onto the empty back page, started to write.

I make no claim to literary merit. Yes, I am an avid reader, but other than a penchant for letters, postcards and greetings at Xmas, my well doesn't exactly runneth over. On this occasion, however, I could not stop. There is usually a lot of time spent waiting about on a film set, and this one with Robert Redford and Deborah Winger was no exception. Applying for a passport shortly after this assignment, I was tempted to fill in the question as to profession by printing: 'Waiting'.

When *Legal Eagles* ended, my scribbling also came to a stop. I hesitate to call it a book. It was an outpouring of memories in close, medium, and long shot that flashed across the silent screen of my mind, just long enough for me to ink them onto the page. The scribbling took the pain away, as if transferring it to another dimension. It was a therapy that got me through the movie; although most days I felt my eyes swollen with unshed tears.

On returning to London, a recent acquaintance, one Xandra Hardie, must have the perused my scribblings on the back of *Legal Eagles* while I busied myself in the kitchen with high tea, and insisted on taking the script with her when she left. Furthermore, she got the ramblings typed and presented them to Liz Calder of the newly-formed Bloomsbury Publishing Company.

Which is how the jottings ended up bound in a book, with almost no effort on my part. In sensitive moments, horizontal in bed descending into sleep or on waking, it made sense to me that my Mum had the wherewithal, even when embarking on the big sleep herself, to give me a last present. I awaited a sign that she had arrived in a safe haven. It is said that the grief tunnel has a duration of two years, but I didn't hear from her. And then, just when I wasn't looking...

22

A rope hanging down to earth

One of the crucial facets in the study of breath with Floris van Pallandt was Hazrat Inayat Khan's division of breath into dense and fine. The dense and audible breath exercises strained the nerves and lungs and helped to develop them and the health of the physical body. But in spiritual development unless the breath be made fine it cannot penetrate through the important centres in the body and cannot reach far enough into the innermost parts of one's life.

He often referred to breath as a bridge between God and man, a rope hanging down to Earth, attached to the Heavens. A rope with the help of which one can climb. In his opinion there was no mystical cult in which breath is not given the greatest importance in spiritual progress. Once a man has touched the depths of his own being with the help of the breath then it becomes easy for him to become one with all that exists on Earth and in Heaven. Breath is the mystery; in it is hidden the secret of life. Breath proves the existence of the life unseen. Breath is audible and at the same time inaudible. Breath is visible and at the same time invisible. It is a certain degree of the activity of the breath and the capacity through which it is acting which makes the breath audible. This shows that there exists something of which we are conscious, the source of which no one knows, which is active every moment of the day, on the model of which the mechanism of nature and art is made. No one can explain whence it came into this mortal body, and no one can say whither it goes when it leaves this body of clay. One can only say that something living came and kept this mortal body alive and left it, proving that the same body which once was thought to be alive, was not really alive, but was itself the life. This proves to the intellect, even those devoid of faith, that there is some source from whence life comes and that it returns to again.

One of the bits of advice George Gurdjieff gave to his students was that if they came across a teaching or even a phrase that resonated with them, to repeat it three times, sometimes aloud. The following is a statement of Hazrat Inayat Khan's that I believe is worthy of just that: 'Man's true self is the part of his being which knows itself to exist, which is conscious of itself. When that self takes breath as its vehicle instead of the body, then it soars upward toward the utmost heights, toward that goal which is the source and origin of all beings.'

23

Thought is the thinker

My pal Jimmy Fraser, who had unearthed me at drama school over twenty-five years earlier, retired. I moved agencies. The new team weren't yet familiar with my anomalies and I was in the habit of dropping into their offices just across the road in Soho. If you don't work regularly, 'out of sight' is often 'out of mind', even if your representation is good.

On one such visit, I was in the agency when the phone rang – actually in the office of an assistant to whom I was chatting. It was an enquiry about my availability. She relayed the details to me as she heard them down the line. There was to be a tribute to Leonard Bernstein in a fortnight, at the Barbican, with the London Symphony Orchestra, to include an array of his compositions, plus a rarely performed work by his early musical guru, Marc Blitzstein, 'The Airborne Symphony', which had not been performed since 1946 in New York. The conductor would be John Mauceri. The full London Symphony Orchestra, opera stars flown in and a choir would participate. Maestro Leonard would be in attendance. The symphony included a narration, the speaking part they hoped I would consider, originally spoken by Orson Welles. It was relayed to me as though I would find the fact inspiring. It had the opposite effect.

Frankly, every new facet relayed to me extended my fear threshold, until it reached critical mass.

Over the years earning my living, I had been compelled to address the fear factor on more than one occasion. The solution I arrived at was to ask myself: 'What are the facts here?'

As I was hearing about the narration of 'The Airborne Symphony', I had the realisation that if I could pull it off I might meet a hero from my seven shows a week at Her Majesty's Theatre, the formidable Leonard Bernstein.

'I'll do it', I heard a voice curiously like my own responding. 'Get the details.'

I stumbled out into Wardour Street and made an escape before my resolve weakened, gulping in air to stop myself from throwing up.

In the arc of a part there is often a click. A keynote that sets the octave for the performance: a pair of shoes that gives the character purchase, a second-hand suit in a thrift store that misfits just right. In this case, the click came in the shape of a bow tie.

Since my first Royal Premiere in 1962, I have always felt comfortable in white tie and tails. In spite of the tailor Doug Hayward, and Dimmie Major, the guy who cut it, coming to my flat to show me how to wear it properly, once I was in it, everything had gone well. Which usually happens when I feel comfortably dressed. So when the Barbican production team asked me what I would prefer to wear, I requested tails. They agreed, even though it meant everyone would have to dress the same. What the hell? Wasn't it in honour of the great Leonard?

George Cleverley, who cut for Rudolph Valentino, Gary Cooper and yours truly

On the other side of Piccadilly where I was living at the time, in the mouth of the small arcade opposite the Royal Academy, is one of the finest men's outfitters in St James. Budd is the shop's name. As soon as I relocated to London's West End from London's East End, I had reconnoitered the village and sampled the best bespoke the capital had to offer. George Cleverley, who made Rudolph Valentino's button-up boots for *Blood and Sand* (he had a thank you letter to prove it), shod my idol Gary Cooper and invented initialed velvet slippers for Winston Churchill, became my shoemaker. Budd made my linen shirts whenever they got their hands on some good stuff; the colours were limited, but I stayed with them until I discovered a Roman shirtmaker who took his own dyes to the old country, where they dyed the Irish linen to order. My future ex-wife once remarked to my tailor: 'He knows more about clothes than acting.' If she had known of the event I am about to relate, her remark would have been more perceptive than flippant.

On the morning in question, young Rollie was on the floor. I explained to him that my tails still fitted but I needed a fresh wing collar. He enquired what I would be doing and I told him. He suggested two objects, the first a period white tie. Unlike the modern variety, it wasn't bow shaped but straight and, whilst it had to be knotted perfectly, drooped elegantly in the style of the Thirties. As the symphony was about the history of flight, culminating with the outbreak of World War II, he felt it would be appropriate. I agreed. The second-hand tie he gave me for a couple of quid. This was the keynote that set the tone of my performance. Yet it was his second brainwave that was to have even deeper ramifications.

One of the problems with the white tie outfit is that the detached stiff collar needs two studs to fix it in place, one back and one front. The back can be visualised as two brass spheres. The outer one is smaller and hinged so that it slides easily through the shirt band and starched collar before it is clicked into its holding position. The front stud is a different design. The base is a sphere, but the end that holds both collar bands of the shirt and both ends of the winged collar is torpedo-shaped for easy penetration through all four layers of material. This design can be seen as a miniature brass capstan no bigger than a fingernail. The whole contraption is covered and further secured when the bowtie is tied in place. Tying a bow was never a problem for me. It was a knack one learned at drama school, as actors in comedies of manners were frequently called upon to tie a bowtie as part of the action, often without a mirror. It was akin to serving tea in china cups without rattling the props.

The second object Mr Rollie suggested was the modern generation of the front collar stud. Instead of the capstan design, it sported two spheres similar to the back stud, but the front, hinged part was the same size as its base button. I saw the sense of it instantly. It would feel more secure. I pocketed my purchases and strolled through the little arcade into Jermyn Street to the best cheese shop in London.

When I address a job, I try to keep it real, dealing with problems whether they be actual or in the mind. The first thing I looked at was redoing a work in Orson's great shadow. The fact was that no one in the audience would have seen his rendition, save Mr Bernstein himself, maybe. That knowledge alone gave me some relief.

I decided to prepare what could be prepared, allay my misgivings about my work, and trust something would happen in the alchemy of the night. I spoke to John Mauceri on the telephone from New York.

'Don't worry', he reassured me. 'I will be in London for the rehearsals.'

'Rehearsals. When?'

'We have two days, one with the orchestra. Plenty of time.'

Plenty of time. A day?

'I don't read music, Maestro', I confessed.

'No problem. I'll bring you in.'

'Could you give me something to listen to? Where the narrator speaks. Preferably not Mr Welles.'

'Yes. Sure. I'll get a tape sent. See you in two weeks.'

He was as good as his word. I received the tape. It wasn't Orson, thank God. A girlfriend of mine lent me her portable tape machine and earphones. It became my constant companion. I ran into Prince Andrew in Burlington Arcade.

'What music you listening to, Terence?' he asked.

I removed an earpiece.

'Learning my words, Your Highness', I replied.

'What a good idea.'

It was. I don't think I have known my wordies so well since my Iago days.

I also enlisted the help of my pal Nickolas Grace. Nik, or 'Amazing', as I call him, is one of those open secrets, for the most part – the genii that frequents the showbiz community in Britain. You may have caught his performance as Anthony Blanche in the original TV version of Evelyn Waugh's *Brideshead Revisited*. He was the character who stuttered so memorably. Nik is the first person I turn to for anything regarding voice or movement. His advice is always of the highest order.

We appeared together in the West End version of Bram Stoker's *Dracula*, where the critics had been intent on driving a stake through the heart of Terence, but ... 'It's a bad wind that blows no one any good', as my Granny Kate used to say.

Nik had plenty of experience with orchestras. He'd sung leads in Gilbert and Sullivan and also several versions of Bernstein's masterpiece, *Candide*. He told me everyone uses microphones these days. Even the rawest of screamers were miked to the max. Educated voices were the minority.

'You'll only need a minute with the mike and the sound engineer – on the day.'

I owned up that I'd had virtually no radio offers to voice jobs that other actors supplement their incomes with, despite the fact that I had worked on the breath from every angle that came my way most days of my working life. And, as I was in the habit of preparing my roles vocally along with everything else, I had the idea that a dialect of English from a bygone age would be fitting. I likened what I was looking for to the voices that I had listened to with my mother on the wireless during the blackout of the Blitz.

I gave him a sample of some of the narrator's lines.

'Are you learning it or reading it?' he wanted to know.

'I don't like it when I am in the audience and a performer reads his lines. There's no eye contact, less empathy.'

'So. You're learning them?'

'Yeah. That's the idea, anyway. I've been working on it a lot.'

'Good. Better.' He paused. 'You know your delivery is perfect RP (received pronunciation). You've managed it without sacrificing the essence of your voice. In fact, all you need to create that wartime delivery is to lean on the "i" vowel.' He considered his advice. 'Yes. That's what you should do – give the "i" full weight.'

He pronounced: 'Evil … the algebra of pure evil.'

It was extremely easy for Amazing. I grimaced

'Look', he said. 'It's extra work, a challenge. Go through the text, underline all the "i" vowels. Evil is good because it is followed immediately by an "l", which you sometimes get lazy with. So, no dark "l"s for Lenny. Hey. You taught me about increasing the need.'

His outings at Sadler's Wells had made him no stranger to staying on the beat.

During the last week before rehearsals, some of my family remarked it was a pity Ethel wasn't around to see this concert. My mother had played piano by ear, the life and soul of the party. None of her offspring inherited her musical gift, another reason she would have appreciated an outing to the Barbican.

My chum Hester, who'd lent me her portable tape player, had been at Ethel's bedside during her final days at Middlesex Hospital. She was my representative amidst the family in my absence, and now she would take my mother's seat at the concert.

Maestro Mauceri arrived. We met. We rehearsed south of the river. He brought me in as promised, once. That evening, my chum Hester made me supper at her place. She asked me if I wanted her to take me through my lines, but I felt it was time I trusted my memory. I had done enough. In those days I was living the food-combining regime, no protein with carbohydrates. That evening, we had salad and rice. During the meal, she commented on the length of my nails.

'Males shouldn't have long nails: it's effeminate', was what she actually said – before setting to work trimming mine.

The day dawned. I awoke in the 10 ½ tatami room that I had constructed for myself on the top floor of my chambers, inspired as I was after my sojourn in Kyoto. The early-April light was glowing through the shoji paper windows. I usually take it easy during the day of a first night. I stretched out on the futon and planned the day backwards, starting from my arrival at the Barbican scheduled for 6.30. I decided to spend some time at the steam baths, like one of my early heroes, Socrates, whose lead bust had graced my chambers from day one.

I got up and extracted my tails from their cover. Placed my Chinese cherry-red amber links and studs halfway through the starchy cuffs and front of the dress shirt. Took the trees out of my black patent shoes and slipped a pair of black silk socks inside them, before putting them back inside the travelling bag that I would carry on the Underground to the Barbican Centre.

Then, I shaved, knees bent, a ritual I had gleaned from a one-hour training session with martial arts master Steve Morris. Obviously sussing my pugilistic abilities within seconds, he did not teach me to fight, but graced me with something far more practical.

'Strengthens the legs while keeping the knees supple.'

In my way of thinking, if in the presence of the greats you expect diamonds but get offered rubies, pick 'em up.

No weak knees tonight … I hoped.

I strolled across the three adjoining parks, only walking across grass, to get to the Queensway Turkish Baths. Halfway across Hyde Park, a large dog detached itself from its owner and bounded over to say hello, only leaving my side when its exasperated master bellowed for it to return. A good omen, was it not.

I leave for the Barbican at 5.45, carrying my performance clothes and 'treading on reality at every step', as they say in Zen enclaves across the world. By 6.30 I arrive at my destination, hang up the outfit in my designated dressing room, itself rather like a monk's cell. Get shown the place where I will sit when not speaking and the microphone when I do. This is a first for me. 'Hi Mike'.

I wave to the sound engineer in the box and give him a level. 'To be or not to be, a very interesting question.'

I Return to my ascetic quarters: practically every surface is carpeted. There are no sharp edges anywhere for a neurotic performer to do himself harm. Perform some light breath work, tongue and voice warm up, courtesy of Julia Wilson-Dickson, or Julia Wilson-Diction, as she was affectionately known at Central Drama School.

At 7.15, I begin to leisurely don my white tie and tails. I am still 'on reality of every step' when I attempt to affix my detached collar. The back stud is easy, as I had put it together before I put the shirt on. The front presents me with a problem. The amber studs in the shirt and waistcoat are in place, but when I attempt to affix the collar itself, only the two starched buttonholes of the shirt and one buttonhole of the collar are accommodated by the newly designed hinged stud. It won't take what is in fact the fourth layer of material. Try as I might, I cannot wrest the second wing of the collar sufficiently over the button to grip the hinge and make it secure. My denuded masculine fingertips are no help whatsoever. I look around the austere room for a tool, a sharp edge, anything. Nothing.

I hear the orchestra tuning up. I look again around the room. Take my shoes from their bags. Slide on my socks. Pull on my shoes, lace them up. Look again at the wayward flying collar in the mirror. Sharp taps on the door! 'Five minutes, Terence.'

A moment of panic followed by a familiar aroma, so faint I almost miss it. Gone before the thought comes. What was that smell? I know it but, no – gone. I realise I am still standing in front of the mirror, which is super-glued to the wall, like everything else. The image that confronts me is lost, helpless. Then several things happen almost at once.

A third cannonade of knocks on my door and, 'Overture and beginners, sir!'

That waft of aroma again. I remember: it is the smell that greeted us on entering the provision store in the town of Yalding when we were hop-picking. It is unique and unmistakable – giant wedges of cheese, freshly baked loaves, spam, bacon, homemade jam, pickles, everything wholesome, unwrapped, on the deep counters of a country store. Yet, how strange is that.

And then an idea slams in. I am a left in a right-handed world. Maybe the collar and stud has a right hand bias. I reverse my hands, still impotently holding the collar and stud. It happens. It's through. It clicks.

'We are ready, sir!'

I deftly tie the white bow. It settles first time.

There's that aroma again, more distinct, it ushers the thought of Ethel to mind.

'I get it, Mum. If you're here, welcome!'

I am through the door. First, up the stairs two at a time. Find my place in front of the microphone. Under my breath: 'Okay, Mike, let's do it.'

I had committed my lines thoroughly to memory, yet the most effort had gone into the opening salvo. If the proscenium arch collapses, my first lines won't desert me. They don't. I hear them, magnified by the electronics, reverberating around the one thousand nine hundred and forty-nine seats of the auditorium. And then it happens, the quiet, an almost imperceptible shift: the air in the immediate vicinity of my nostrils becomes duvet soft. The centre of my being is expanding; a heightened sensitivity that takes in the whole room. It could also be an inrush of the energy in the auditorium that my consciousness, aware of its own mirror-like quality, is spontaneously reflecting.

The thought arrives. Yes, there is thought, yet no thinker.

Question: What to do?

Immediately, I have a mental picture of a clasped hand concealing a thumb. What's concealed? If the hand is spread, it is empty. If kept closed, there may be something in it. No one knows for sure.

Answer: Nothing.

The words continue their flow. The action continues, yet there is no 'one' acting. Thoughts arise without a thinker. There is only the seamless interaction of sound and listening.

Midpoint is traversed. My practiced line: 'The algebra of pure evil.'

From somewhere, I hear the weighted 'i', the undark 'l'. Perfect. I congratulate myself. My mind is working. I'm thinking. Boy, that sounded good.

Silence. The orchestra has stopped.

'Somebody's forgot a cue', I say to myself.

I glance about me. John Mauceri is staring directly at me, his baton raised.

Oh my god! It's me!

His baton begins its downward swing.

'It begins!' I just manage to squeeze the words in under its arc.

The background of abundance shining and full, shrivelled, gone as lonely Terence steps backward, slumps onto his chair, winded. Thoughts overwhelm me.

The silence is gone.

The symphony continues. Vanity, thy name is Stamp.

What to do? Pull yourself together. Or make a start at least. I bow my head and look at my shiny black shoes. Let's put the energy in the feet. How do the feet feel? I wrinkle my toes. How is the stage actively feeling tonight? Now. Just now.

A moment before my next cue, I stand and step back into the fray. As I begin, it returns, the shift, the peaceful energy – the background always there, rarely noticed.

The symphony ends. Heartfelt applause. We all gather backstage: 'Us happy few.' Maestro Bernstein enters, with much aplomb. He sees me and extends his arms. We meet halfway. He encircles me in his hug. Places his mouth close to my ear and whispers, 'You missed a cue.'

His words reverberate.

My chum Hester has driven to the performance in her BMW. She drives me home. We park in the forecourt at Albany. She switches off the car and sits facing the Georgian mansion. The headlights of passing traffic in Piccadilly illuminate auburn shafts of her hair.

'What happened?'

'When?'

'When you dried. When you sat down, dropped your head.'

'Oh. I lost the flow. Just trying to get myself together. Why do you ask?'

'I saw your mother's face, on yours. I blinked. And it vanished.'

I could not answer. There is too much and nothing to say.

The next day the agency rings. 'We've had an ad executive on the blower. Wants to try your ... expensive voice for the new campaign.'

Is this coincidence? My mother? Or the Oneness of vibration?

24

The *Lady from the Sea* and her stranger

In 1977 I was lured back to the stage to play *Dracula* in the play of the same name. It was a splendid production designed in just black and white. It opened at the Shaftesbury Theatre. The critics didn't approve. We closed after four weeks. I thought, oh well, stick to what you do best, Terence, and carried on in celluloid. The one good thing that came out of the debacle was meeting and working with Nickolas Grace. We've remained chums ever since. Most of the public recognise him as the gay with the stammer in Michael Lindsay-Hogg and Charles Sturridge's television production of *Brideshead Revisited*.

However, that same year I was approached by the director Michael Elliott, arguably the best and most sympathetic at work in the theatre. He worked predominantly with the Manchester Exchange Theatre Group where his production of Ibsen's *Lady from the Sea* had opened. He intended to restage it in-the-round at the Roundhouse in Camden, with Vanessa Redgrave. The cast would remain unchanged save for the role of the Stranger, the unworldly character who appears out of the ether and causes changes. The actor who worked in Manchester is unavailable.

One meeting with Michael Elliott convinced me to give it a go, and I justified my decision by telling myself it was worth the risk to exit stage left on an up.

Superficially the differences between Vanessa and myself were philosophical. Michael Elliott was more than sensitive enough to harmonize our differing concepts.

Watching Vanessa work I could see the great name of Redgrave in action. The nobility I had so admired in her father, Sir Michael.

Things revved up when we took up residence in the great space in Camden. The old converted train shed was much favoured by musicians but looked upon with ambivalence by actors. Being viewed in-the-round one feels on show or exposed, either way it involved a shift in the presence gears for yours truly. Also on my mind was what I had worked so hard for hadn't impressed many in the Shaftesbury. Could I pull this off and hold my line? Ibsen's 'Stranger' was written to be other-worldly, set apart from the other residents in the action. Yes, it was working OK on celluloid; the silver element of which film is based ideally suited my orientation.

The opening night could not have gone better. On the circular stage the energy surrounded us, enclosing and energising us. I understood instantly why Vanessa is credited with being one of our great actresses. Her presence and focus are pure, uninterrupted. Our connection, yin and yang, seamless.

Michael Elliott was overjoyed and praised the whole cast. Fleet Street agreed.

Jim Carrey and the Yes Man

Yes Man was a great job for me. Not only was it a funny film, it had the added plus of working with one of moviedom's top comedy actors, Jim Carrey. He is also a delight to be with, and never late on set. We had so much to chat about and the topic of comedy timing never came up. Yet I felt good working with such a comic artist and holding my end up.

Shortly after the eventful happenings at the Barbican and my portrayal of The Monitor in 'The Airborne Symphony', Michael Cimino was reputedly in London casting around for his production of *The Sicilian*. It was the gossip of the acting community. I heard from two guys that it was mayhem in the offices where he was seeing people, as he frequently got into lengthy discussions, causing a build-up of tried and tested actors who could do nothing but wait and talk amongst themselves. One told me it was like a meat market.

My eight-year sabbatical following *The Mind of Mr Soames* in 1969 had more than erased any ideas I had of seeing myself predominantly as a leading man; still, despite a great respect for Mr Cimino, I didn't feel ready to join a queue.

Time passed, I didn't push it one way or the other with my agents, and more or less forgot about any chance I might have had with *The Sicilian*.

Until, one morning, while seated in Fortnum and Mason's Soda Fountain at the same table where my mother and I often used to take our afternoon tea, Michael Stevenson entered my life.

Michael Stevenson is something of a legend in the film game. There isn't anything – or anyone – he doesn't know. And while his resume lists his array of skills – among them line producer, co-producer, third assistant, second assistant, first assistant, personal assistant – most will know him as the finest second assistant in the business, bar none. This is his chosen role. He is frequently bought off films in production and sequestered onto others that perhaps have a difficult star.

Mr Stevenson loves actors and they love him. He is a gentle man in the original sense of the word; all the more impressive as his gentleness is born of strength. He claims to have taken after his mother, and it isn't well known outside of East London circles that his father was John Stevenson (or Tiger Stevenson, which was the name he fought under), one of the very last pugilists to fight in the bare-knuckle ring. One of his last bouts was at the Hoxton Town Hall against the fearsome father of Ronnie and Reggie Kray. This contest was called a draw after fifty or so punishing rounds. After the fight was stopped, the two combatants continued their fisticuffs in the street, to the delight of the home-going crowd.

A rematch at the famous venue Blackfriars was scheduled, yet never fought, as bare-knuckle fighting was outlawed. A famous pub now occupies the bloodstained site. Tiger lived to be ninety-three and, when in his eighties, five youths tried to push past him as he was getting off a number nine Routemaster and took exception to the old age pensioner standing his ground. They set about teaching him a lesson. He knocked out four and the fifth ran away.

His son Michael had been in the film game almost as long as myself. He was always the first of the crew on board whenever David Lean or

Stanley Kubrick began a film, as his knowledge of artists and technicians is encyclopaedic.

It was late in April, and I was in the Soda Fountain, trying to write a sequel to my first book, *Stamp Album*. It was a quiet morning and I had the place almost to myself when Michael came in.

He introduced himself, and then his colleagues: Cimino, and Joanna, his producer. After I had assured them they weren't disturbing me, they sat down.

I later learned they had seen most of the actors in town and were on their way to Heathrow in a black cab when Cimino asked the other Michael if there were any actors of note they hadn't seen. He mentioned me and informed them he might know a place en route to the airport where I could be found. And so it was I wound up in Sicily a month later, playing a prince.

Michael Stevenson met my late flight into Sicily himself—a thirty-mile drive. He'd have no strange non-English speaking driver holding a board for 'Mr Stump', not on a Michael Stevenson shoot.

On the lengthy ride of the location, Michael explained to me that Cimino encouraged his cast to really get into their parts, and billeted them accordingly. Actors playing mafia fraternized with mafia; actors playing police hung out with policemen. As I was Prince Borsa, he wanted me to stay in the best hotels and had fixed it for me to meet up with some local Sicilian aristocrats. However, the producer who had contracted me for the whole shoot balked at paying so much in the way of expenses, so Cimino paid for my stay out of his own pocket.

During my first day on set, the extras were, for the most part, real people. In Sicily, no one is ever identified as mafia, and when the aristocrats arrived for hair and make-up, the Countess, whose father had been the model for my part, addressed me as Prince Borsa. Then, turning to face the others in the room, she exclaimed, 'Oh, you must be playing the Mafioso!'

Most of the long hauls from location to location were overland, and the longest of the shoot was when we travelled to Agrigento. The trip took most of the day. When we arrived, the transport manager met our car and explained to me that contrary to the director's wishes, the hotel outside which we were standing was all he could get for me at present. He said he was still looking, but the town was a tourist site as it boasted an almost complete temple built by the ancient Greeks, and good rooms were hard to find.

The hotel was tacky, especially after the luxury to which I had become accustomed. But as my chum Baron Frederik said on more than one occasion: 'Aristocrats and working class can turn their hands to anything, even if it entails unblocking a lavatory.'

With this in mind, I lay down on the grimy candlewick bedspread that covered the narrow bed and tried to relax, but the window was open and the screams from the pool directly beneath it were non-stop: it was obviously a stopover for tour buses. Late afternoon – it was too early for supper, too late for a nap. Besides, there was no chance of falling asleep with the racket outside from the kids' impromptu swim competition – or so I thought.

Film shoots, especially on location, are always tough, and before long I felt very weary and laid my head back against the lumpy pillow.

In 1942, when Mum and I moved from my gran's house, spacious on a wide road, with a garden and a cellar, I took an instant dislike to the downsizing. It was a two-up two-down, a scullery (a small room with a single sink), no bathroom, an outdoor loo and a small yard in which nothing ever grew. To make matters worse, unbearable sometimes, a low wooden fence separated it from the most scrumptious garden I had ever seen. While ours could be measured in feet, our neighbour's house could only be glimpsed beyond the lawns, shrubs, climbing roses, and pear trees only an arm's reach from our grasp – conference pears whose rusty skins ripened and dropped unnoticed every autumn. Except by us, of course. Held in check by a low-slung plank fence we were strictly forbidden to straddle.

The only room in 124 Chadwin Road that I genuinely liked was our bedroom, which looked out on the street. It also overlooked the only other feature I approved of: our front step, a design of square tiles, red, black and beige. It fell to me to keep them clean, snow, rain or sun. When Mum fell pregnant with our sister, the longed-for daughter to add to the trio of sons, a new anteroom was constructed by my father Tom at one side of their bedroom – which was larger – into which we boys were relocated. I hated it.

The bizarre thing about Chadwin Road, which I was happy to abandon in my haste to move 'up West', was that I periodically dreamed of returning there. These dreams took on an importance when they began to feature regularly in my adult life. When my mother's Mum died, my beloved Granny Perrott, and she was finding her life a bit too much to bear, Granny Perrott would invariably manifest to her in her dreams. Whilst she wouldn't remember any specifics, she always woke up revived and feeling empowered, anew.

My dreams, the sensible ones, had a decal. They always began with me standing on the front step looking down at the harlequin design I had taken care of as a boy. Once I entered the front door I could be anywhere, yet the dreams always opened on the red, black and biscuit tiles.

And so it happens in Agrigento. No sooner have I closed my eyes than I am once again outside 124 looking down at the adorned doorstep. I knock on the windows of the front door. They're covered in the jolly Christmas paper we had stuck on them one winter. We'd left it on as it made our front door windows resemble stained glass. No one answers. This is not right. I have to get in. Knock again. No answer. Momentarily, I'm stumped. Then I decide to walk around the corner, maybe to visit the local park, Beckton Park, where it is said seven winds blow.

I turn right, right again. Take the third turning into the main road, walking along the pavement opposite the park with its lido and old plane trees.

I pass number 353; a curtain in the front window moves, catching my side vision. I turn. The curtain is held back, revealing my mother. She beckons me. I walk to the front door, which she opens. I enter. 'What are you doing? It's not our house.'

She's walking ahead of me. She turns and smiles. I follow her, out into the garden. It is as I remember it but more splendid. I haven't ever seen it from here. I smell scented flowers, lilac. The grass and leaves are silvery. The Straffon's privet tree is in bloom, the aroma heavy. She walks ahead, with me right behind her. I see our house; the wooden fence is gone and the splendour has spilled over into our yard. 'This is all ours, now', she explains.

We enter the scullery door. Speaking as she leads me up the narrow staircase. It is dark, as always. 'I know you didn't like the back bedroom, but I want to show it to you.'

We are inside the bedroom, which now has as its view the combined grounds, fruit trees and all.

In the fashion of dreams, all the family is suddenly in the room. We all look out of the window. Yet I sense danger. Carefully, I lead everybody back to the ground floor. I am right. The whole bedroom is collapsing.

My mother is unperturbed. She assures me: 'Don't be sorry. Things are simple to fix here. Come look!' She rolls back a carpet from the floor in the middle of the living room, the same carpet that I spent hours lying on in front of the fire. I grew in a horizontal position. Hence my father's nickname for me, 'the horizontal champ'.

She raises a trap door in the floor that I never knew existed. It has delicate piano hinges.

She invites me closer. I see a wooden slide, like in a playground, incredibly smooth, a fine yellow wood. She urges me to inspect the space. I slip down it into a small room that is awash with glowing tribal carpets, woven from muted colours. Her voice becomes softer, conspiratorial. I can no longer see her, yet her welcoming words are close to my ear. 'I made it for you. So you know you always have a place. A home. It will always be here for you. Wherever you are. Your real home.'

I lay on the carpets, in the position I laid in as a youth in front of the fire. I feel I'm rising, almost levitating on an even plane. Hear the tweeting of birds. Sense the dream landscape has faded.

I am back in the hotel on the candlewick bedspread. The shouts of enthusiasm and splashing have stopped. I can hear birds close by. I open my eyes. I am looking at the open windows. Near the corner of the outside mantel is affixed a nest, from the top of which I see tiny beaks. It is these from which the chirping is emanating. A swallow flies in with its beak full; it apportions its haul into the babies' open mouths. How did I not see this before?

The telephone is ringing. I pick it up. It's the film's transport manager. 'Hi, Terence, I have found you a nicer hotel. I am organising transport. Come down in ten minutes.'

The new digs are wonderful, with a generous ground-floor room and tall doors opening onto a terrace, which itself has a view of the ancient acropolis.

I am out of the grief tunnel. My mother has landed somewhere.

25

The present is the eternal

He is austere without harshness. We sit in silence for some time.

Finally, he says: 'Haven't seen you in any films lately.'

'My films don't pull in big audiences. As it happens, my public is almost as small as yours.'

This draws a chuckle. 'It's true.'

'Why is that?'

'It's like what we were talking about at Brockwood; people choose to live superficially. They have a vested interest in thought. Years, lifetimes, centuries. Can't give it up or rather can't see beyond it.'

I try a different tack.

'It's known you don't like to talk about yourself, but I feel we've known each other a long time.' He doesn't appear to object, so I press on. 'I heard you like motorbikes.'

'No', he replies, 'cars, fast cars.'

I take a deep breath. 'Before this happened to you.'

I am thinking of the pepper tree, August 1922. 'What were you like?'

'I was an idiot.' Then he corrects himself and, letting his jaw slacken, he pulls it down. 'No, I was gormless. No thought in the head. My parents would give me money, I would give it to the first beggar who asked. They would send me out for a walk, I would just keep walking. That's why they had my little brother keep an eye on me. When the realisation came that the mind could observe itself, there were no distracting thoughts. It all occurred rather quickly.'

'I find that depressing', I said.

'Why?'

'Well, it's been nearly twenty years since our paths crossed. I sweated through your books, tried to stay alert during your talks, always assuming you had a radio in your head, always on. Now you tell me you're not a free diver, you are a fish.'

His voice segued into its minor key. 'You don't have to be Edison to switch on the electric light.'

'Listen ...' I said. He reaches out. His hand on my arm warm and dry.

'Just be aware when you are unaware. Then the mind is sharpening itself.' He smiles the serene smile. How could I not believe him?

26

'I read the news today oh boy'

Krishnamurti's passing
17th February, 1986

Had I known the aforementioned meeting with Krishnaji was to be the last time I would be graced with his presence, I can't say I would have been more attentive; it was one of the unique qualities of being with him that the quality of his being raised yours to his. From the first, 'Look at that tree' to 'You don't have to be Edison ... '

And from what Mary Zimbalist writes in her diary of the final days spent with him, this is apparent.

On the 3rd February he sat in a wheelchair near the pepper tree where he could see the hills. He asked to be alone there and sat motionless and silent. 'It was absolutely as clear as daylight that Krishnaji was saying goodbye to the hills, goodbye to the mountains.'

On the evening of the 15th February she had washed his hair and was massaging almond oil into his scalp. 'I was holding in my hands this warm and beautiful head that holds the brain that is the light of the world. It is there, alive, marvellous, beyond my knowing. The source of his teaching is an endless giving.'

Caroline Bliss-Seycombe (a Miss Moneypenny)

27

Just keep saying 'yes', probably it will go away

Caroline Bliss is an actress. We met in Manchester in 1984. It can be a complicated process, friendship between performing artists. Usually, only staying in the business ensures that paths cross.

Yet it proved easy with Caroline. Shortly after we met she landed a part in the West End, and Albany, where I was living at the time, was directly on her flight path to the Comedy Theatre, which she reported to six days a week. In between shows on Wednesdays we'd have a cuppa. At one such tea break she commented how harmonious my apartment was. As she is a very smart girl, I waited for the other shoe to drop, which it duly did.

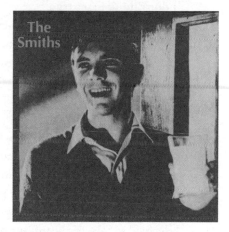

The Smiths

Enduring Relevance

'I can see why you don't go out much ... '

I did my best to smile encouragingly.

'Of course, when you were working regularly, you naturally put yourself about, but nowadays nobody seems to see you. Everyone I meet who knows I know you is curious.'

'Really?'

'Most think you're a recluse. Of course, I'm happy to lie on your behalf ... '

'So, you think I'm a recluse?'

'Well, hardly anyone gets to see you these days.'

'Except you.'

'I'm pushy.'

'I invited you to tea.'

'And very good it is, too.'

I was serving an organic white from the right side of the hill.

'Listen, Caroline, as we are fellow Cancerians, you can cut to the chase; otherwise you'll be late for the half and I'll have to wait till next week for the payoff.'

She luxuriated in the needlepoint Bergere armchair it had taken years to complete.

'You should work more.'

'Easier said than done. I don't like to do crap unless I haven't got the rent.'

'Yes. Sure. But you've manipulated your agent to such a degree, she probably doesn't even show you most of the offers that come in.'

'I don't think that's true.'

'It's easy to check. Tell the agency you want to read more. Better: tell them you want to do comedies – to look out for comedic subjects.'

Caroline was not someone whose opinion I took lightly.

'I can do that.'

'Promise?'

'Promise.'

On reflection, a lot of what she had said did resonate with me. I had put a lot of restrictions on the team: No long runs in the theatre. No TV. No first time directors. No films being shot in Australia (I'd had a really horrible introduction to the paparazzi and Melbourne matrons on my first trip in '66, accompanying a girlfriend to the Melbourne Cup).

I decided to take my agent out to lunch in order to fulfil my promise to Caroline.

The agency at the time was north of Oxford Street and comprised of three floors above a shop. I pressed the doorbell, announced myself and was buzzed in. My destination being the top floor, I set about climbing the steep stairs. But on the first floor landing, the partner agent, Stephanie Randall, who'd obviously overheard my well-produced announcement, opened her office door, brandishing a rolled-up script like a tennis racquet (she is a member of the All England Lawn Tennis and Croquet Club) and proclaimed: 'This has just arrived. It's a comedy. About drag queens.'

I looked about me as though someone within earshot had blown my intention.

'D'you want me to give it a proper once-over or d'you want to read it?' she continued.

It was beyond coincidence. I hadn't even let on about my tentative change of outlook.

'I'll read it. Thanks, Steph.'

I didn't. It wasn't from lack of trying. Yet every time I opened the script, usually sat on my bespoke, untreated hide settee, I only ever managed to scan a few pages before being overcome by an irresistible fatigue, which I inevitably succumbed to.

Days passed. Wednesday rolled around. In between shows at the Comedy Theatre, Miss Bliss arrived for our picnic. I had been the recipient of some small leaf Tarry Souchong mailed by a friend and was keen to hear what my fellow tea aficionado made of it. Pointing to her favourite chair, I pottered off into the kitchen to get started on the ritual, paying little regard to the screenplay on the circular Chinese table, where I intended to serve the new brew.

Minutes later I do.

While Caroline poured, the telephone rang.

I answered. It was Steph, from the agency. 'Hello, darling. I was wondering if you'd had a chance to look at that screenplay?'

I should mention that Stephanie Randall was trained by the great voice teacher Rudi Shelley at the Bristol Old Vic School in the Sixties; he had all his pupils 'speak up' (meaning, loudly) whenever possible.

'Yes. Yes. I have looked at it.' Not untrue. I had looked at it. I just hadn't managed to finish it.

'What d'you think?'

'Well, it's a bit of a one-joke piece, isn't it? "Cocks in frocks".' Caroline had carefully placed her bowl of tea back on the tray and was looking in my direction.

'Oh', said the big voice on the telephone. 'We all rather liked it.'

At the time, there was only one male employed at the agency and he handled the accounts. So the 'we' was a rather loaded plural. The significance of which was not lost on me, yet my attention was divided as the guest in my direct line of vision was obviously trying to get my attention, pointing a still forefinger in much the same way her grandfather pointed his baton, her remarks overlapping Stephanie's.

'Say yes. And hang up', was all I heard.

'What?' I asked.

'Sorry, darling, is somebody there?' said Stephanie.

'No. No, it's okay, Steph.'

'Say yes and hang up', Caroline repeated with increased intent.

Stephanie, apparently hearing a feminine voice in the room: 'Terence, look, if this is a bad time ... '

'No. No.'

'Tell her yes. And hang up.'

Appearing contrite, but actually confused, I said into the telephone, 'Listen, Steph, why don't we ... er ... progress it. If you all like it ... '

I could tell by the less strident response that my agent felt she had compromised me into a position I wouldn't normally take.

'Oh, darling, he's not very experienced, the director. It's very low budget, no money to speak of and ... it shoots in ... Australia.'

'Progress it, Steph. Talk to you soon.'

I hung up and focused my scrutiny on Miss Bliss.

'What?'

She waved to the script next to the tea, which she'd obviously had a sneaky peek at while I was in the kitchen.

'It's a drag film, three queens in a bus going across the outback', I said. Caroline doesn't scoff, but if she did her reaction would be close.

'What?' I challenged.

'Your reaction is what is interesting.'

'My reaction?'

'Yes. Or to put it bluntly ... your fear is out of proportion to the project.'

I was about to take her up on that when I recalled the sleepiness I had felt every time I tried to get through the piece.

'It's your reaction you should be looking at,' she said.

I kept my mouth shut. She continued.

'It's simple really. Just keep saying "Yes". Probably it will go away. Then fine. If it doesn't, somewhere along the line what is so frightening will become clear and you can address it. It's not a career move; it's a growth move.'

She then devoted herself to her tea.

Which is more or less what happened. I kept on taking in deep breaths and letting out shallow quavering "yesses" while Caroline provided me with unyielding support. Discovering esoteric groups that provided shelter wherein individuals were encouraged to practice life in symmetry with the motions of their hearts. And, finally, expeditions to shoe stores that catered for the more sizeable of women.

On entering the first of these, the salesman had asked us what size we needed. Caroline had looked at me. I had said to her: 'eleven'. 'Eleven', she repeated.

'We don't do small sizes', the salesman responded.

'They're for him!' she said.

She also reported for tea with make-up and loose dresses so I could get used to the look and feel in private.

28

Thought is the thinker

I, Bernadette, find myself standing on top of a high, narrow pub bar in a mined-out mining town Down Under named Broken Hill – waiting to lead my fellow drag queens into an alternative rendering of 'Shake Your Groove Thing'.

I am conscious of the steamroller of mindless vapouring steaming through my brain. 'What are you doing here? You're a middle-aged man. You were the benchmark Iago of Webber-Douglas. The best dressed man in England. You're a closet philosopher. You've sat with wise men. You're ... '

'Camera. Playback. ACTION!'

The intro of 'Shake Your Groove thing' blares over the sound system. DA-DA-DA-DA-DI-DA-DA.

My mind stops. I sense my lips moving, syncing the blaring words, my body gyrating—

Like I have stopped out of time. Suddenly: 'Cut! Print!'

The take is over. We've done it.

Fear? Yes, there was plenty of fear, a kaleidoscope of projections of being made to look nakedly silly. It was my core dread and, ironically, that was exactly what the role demanded.

'Next setup', I hear the director say.

And me? I'm silent, unmoving, existing in that place one finds when dread is faced and fear temporarily banished. I'd like to stay here but ...

The Australia I experienced was indeed another county from the one abandoned in the Sixties. The troupe and fellow artists were first class. It wouldn't be a porky to say I could never have pulled Priscilla off without Hugo Weaving, Guy Pearce, Bill Hardy and the rest of the team.

The initial days were light for me, and the transition from costume, wig fittings, and choreography went smoothly. Of course, the director had Hugo, Guy and me out on the town in full drag, an interesting sight. On leaving my hotel to meet at Hugo's house to get dressed and made up, I said to the night manager, 'I may look different when I come back – feminine. It's for a movie.'

'They all say that', she retorted.

What I hadn't paid enough attention to was the virtually impossible task of performing in a synchronised dance trio while simultaneously keeping perfect lip sync with the musical lyrics blasting out of the playback. I had been given a tape of the numbers us gals were to perform and been asked to learn them. The dance master had drilled us religiously on the steps of the routines. We hadn't actually rehearsed combining the two. This oversight became crystal clear on the morning of the first routine, when we were shown the set in Broken Hill, and shuffled along the narrow dance space at 6 am before reporting to hair and make-up.

As the only member of the cast who was not Australian, I had been honoured with my own trailer. Guy and Hugo shared the other.

In solitary splendour and fully made up, I got into drag.

I was beginning to feel my nerves as I put my long fake thumbnail through my fishnet tights, then bellowing out for Tim Chappel, who was Lizzie Gardiner's brilliant collaborator.

He entered, holding an electric razor to his half-shorn chest. 'What is it, doll?'

'I'm sorry, Tim. I laddered my tights. Give us another pair, mate.'

'Can't.'

'Come on. I know it's a small budget, but a pair of tights … '

'It's not that. They're Queenies (made for extra-large girls), difficult to find in Sydney. Impossible in Broken Hill.' He pulled a face. 'Show me.'

I indicated the gaping ladder in my tights. He shrugged.

'Forget it', he advised. 'It's drag. It's meant to be tacky.'

I was alone with my besmirched Queenies and nausea erupted in my gut. I wasn't sure if I could get out of my wagon.

Suddenly there was a 'c-o-o-o-e-e-e!' from outside. It sounded like Hugo and Guy. I opened my door and peered out. It was. They were arm in arm, like two girls about to leave a group to go and freshen up. They smiled in unison.

'We thought we'd go in together. They're ready on set.'

And so I found myself atop that perilously narrow bar. A harsh ginger wig with detachable pigtails, laddered tights, star-spangled knickers, high-heeled dancing shoes, amongst a room full of out of work miners who'd been plied with beer to keep them from leaving.

What Bernadette taught me once and for all was that fear is only ever thought.

In closing, I should tell you that just before I got to see the film of Priscilla for the very first time – a midnight screening at the Cannes Film Festival – I received a telephone call from the Director of Photography. He was mumbling and seemed to be apologising to me for his lighting job on my character, Bernadette, during the film.

'You didn't do well by me – why?'

'It was Steph', he explained. 'I told him "he's gotta face for camera. Will only need a little front light". "No", he said, "I don't want him looking good." I'm really sorry, Terence.'

So there I was, dressed to the nines for my first midnight premiere at Cannes. The lights dimmed. The curtain went up; the film began; I was about to view my creation, Bernadette, my androgynous inspiration, a woman trapped inside the body of a man.

I took a luxurious breath in anticipation of the filmic results of my emotional rollercoaster, inspired by the wonderful females who had enriched my life: Christie, Shrimpton, Mangano, Princess Diana – any and all of whom I would be happy to be in a female incarnation, but no, up there on the giant silver screen looking back at me was an old tomcat. By royal appointment of Stephan Elliott.

Vanity, thy name is Terence.

29

'A blinder,' the Princess concluded.

One of the charms of having followed a profession for many years is to be able to look back and see where the seeds of future events were sown, albeit seemingly unimportant at the time. It began with Ken Loach's 1966 movie *Poor Cow*.

Loach liked to fill his productions with actual characters, which was how Carol and I came to work with John Bindon, a real life tealeaf cast to play

a tealeaf (thief) – and Carol's common law husband – in the piece. No problem for yours truly, for whilst Bindon had a reputation as a notorious hard case, he was a complete gentleman on set, comical too, and also notorious for his prodigious appendage – what Marlon Brando would have termed his 'noble tool'.

In fact, he had a trick that he was fond of performing in public, which involved flashing this massive wherewithal. He would unzip his Strides, whip it out and, clasping the trunk with both hands, twirl the uncut policeman's helmet a few times before safely returning it to his ample trousers and zipping up. I bore witness to this one afternoon while strolling along with him on Kings Road in Chelsea. Walking toward us was the famed reformist peer Lord Longford. Bindon spotted him, nudged me, and in the blink of an eye completed his party trick. So fast and so obviously well-rehearsed that I had trouble believing what I had just seen, yet the expression on the great and good's face conveyed the disoriented bewilderment of someone whose gin and tonic had been laced with LSD.

I heard at a later date that Bindon had been a guest on the Caribbean island of Mustique, along with the great fashion photographer Richard Avedon, who persuaded him to air his gyration for fellow vacationer Princess Margaret and her entourage as she came down from her suite to join the group for cocktails. Reputedly, Avedon offered to snap the event. Bindon couldn't resist.

'A blinder', the Princess concluded.

'I've seen bigger in Malaya', the lady-in-waiting added.

Later still, Bindon stood trial for the murder of an equally fearsome hard case, Johnny Dark.

In his testimony, John recounted the details of the knifing for the court. The curious judge interjected, 'Are you saying, Mr Bindon, you actually intended to knife Mr Dark to death?'

'That's right.'

'But why on earth, man?'

'Well, he was actually trying to kill me at the time, Your Honour.'

He received an in-self-defence verdict.

You can see why it wasn't hard to stay in character with the likes of Bindon on the set.

The other reality check was the fact that Ken Loach improvised the whole film. I am certain he knew precisely what he was doing, but we didn't have a script. He always shot scenes between Carol and me using two cameras simultaneously. This proved to be a once in a lifetime opportunity for me, but it certainly didn't feel like it on the first day. Method acting it wasn't. No 'emotional memory' appropriate here.

I had moved on from the Method of trying to re-live emotional moments, tethered as they were in the past, but hadn't actually discovered any modus operandi with a more dynamic slant. Suddenly without preparation or the constraints of learned dialogue, and not knowing what Carol would say or do between 'Action' and 'Cut', it became a discipline of 'empty head' on 'Action'. Causing me to realise that performance is as spontaneous as speaking is in real life. All that is required is the firm belief that whatever arises from the stillness that underlies all motion would be organically connected to the moment.

Cut to 1998, Kauai, the Hawaiian island. On holiday in a basic beach hotel whose rooms have no telephones. A message is left at reception to ring Steven Soderbergh at an 818 number in California. I collect a handful of quarters and find my way to a public open-air phone on the beach. Dial the number, and in a minute am connected to the young maestro whose first film, *Sex, Lies and Videotape*, made such a big impression on the business – and me. Would I be interested in playing in a gangster movie entitled *The Limey*? He also mentioned the

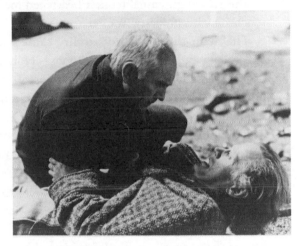

Peter Fonda with The Limey

possibility of using footage from an earlier film I had appeared in, *Poor Cow*, as a kind of back-story.

To be frank, I was lost for words and didn't respond.

'So, what d'you think?' he asked, after a long pause.

'Yes!!'

'Oh, great.' He sounded relieved.

It was my turn to ask a question:

'Tell me, Stephen. Was there ever any doubt?'

'Oh, sure. It's not many leading men who relish being up there with their thirty years' younger selves.'

So it began.

My first and only meeting with Steven, prior to signing, took place in the garden of the Chateau Marmont, in Los Angeles. He told me that when you looked at most people, you could imagine cogs turning in their heads. What he wanted to feel from Wilson, my character, was the presence of a bigger cog behind the others, moving in increments, but powering their motion.

Later, after I'd committed, he rang me. Could I work out what Wilson would wear? He didn't know much of English fashion.

Both of these seeming flecks of direction created a lot of reverberation for me. In fact, they were all the tips I needed.

This seemingly casual request heartened me a great deal. I'm always touched by his modesty, as its charm is its

The main thrusts of my vitality came with the realisation that Soderbergh and co-writer Lem Dobbs – 'Holy cow - *Poor Cow* - check it out!' was the memo he'd sent Stephen after re-discovering the old film – had constructed the Limey with me in mind; I was determined to plumb the depths and scale the heights to justify their faith. Wilson would speak as my own father had. Wilson's body would tilt forward like the author Ian Fleming, whose bearing struck me as leaning into life. It was a veritable 'Life of Riley' to have a character I'd given birth to thirty years previous to tether my present day Limey to, and an absolute luxury to work with a great director at a time in my life when I knew enough to appreciate one. I've heard it said that Soderbergh doesn't consider himself a storyteller, more of a technician fascinated by the intricacies of film itself.

You could have fooled me.

I prepared in the crisp fresh air of Vancouver, memorizing the script until the words became second nature, while hardening up at the wonderful Diane Miller's Pilates studio, using the form of exercise developed by boxer-gymnast Joe Pilates nearly a hundred years ago. Based on muscular control as well as development, Pilates promotes a strong, functional body. There are some things you just can't act. And no amount of period whistle (a Sixties suit) would convey a prison-tough body if there wasn't one underneath. Or the 'big cog' that Soderbergh suggested far behind the eyes.

Steven used his handheld, lightweight Arriflex, marking one of the few times in a very long career that my gal (the camera) and the director were not two. Dialogue preparation combined with the spontaneity of the director resulted in the same impromptu spur-of-the-moment feel achieved on the *Poor Cow* shoot, and also bears witness to Steven's highly developed intuition, in not only his sparing use of the old footage, but featuring it in black-and-white, a stark and melancholic contrast to the Limey of his creation.

Later, at a film festival in Rotterdam, Holland, I do a Q and A on stage following a screening. A local babe asks me, 'Where's the guy who played the young Wilson?'

Appreciating her inferred wantonness and the amazing legs a lot of Dutch girls have, I catch myself feeling nostalgic for my own twenty-five-year-old physique. With a sigh I respond, 'He had his fifteen minutes of fame. I haven't heard from him lately.'

30

True presence seems empty yet it is fully present

One of the problems for a performer hoping to trust intuition when it comes to deciding which projects to go with, obviously preferable to having no project to choose from, is fear. The entrance of fear is always thought, and the speed of thought can be super-fast. It goes without saying as one is usually unmindful of thought and its vagaries, one is consumed by it before one is aware of it.

Listening to the wisdom of Tim Burton

That's what happened when I was approached about the film *A Song for Marion*, written by Paul Andrew Williams and also to be directed by him. It was such a fine screenplay that my new agent Lindy King had no reservations about getting it straight to me. The role on offer was a married man whose wife has contracted cancer. The name of the character was Arthur and the main arc or sweep of the story was about a man trying to find his voice, which is a subject that has intrigued me for almost as long as I have been interested in performing.

Fear entered the picture with the realisation that the success of the film was dependent on the climax in the final scene, the Billy Joel ballad sung by Arthur. I couldn't convince myself that I could pull it off. Time passed as my dithering persisted. I was then informed that Vanessa Redgrave had accepted the part of Marion.

I don't know if I have mentioned this before, but a very negative influence in my early career, one James Woolf, a producer, convinced me of, or rather enforced, my fears about accepting the role of King Arthur in the musical *Camelot*, as my singing voice would probably have to be voiced by a more proficient singer. When the film was premiered and I heard how Richard Harris had made a success with his voice, I always regretted my decision. When I heard Vanessa had been cast, all I could think of was that she had been King Arthur's wife in *Camelot* and now she would be playing another Arthur's wife in *Song for Marion*. Was the universe offering up a second chance?

I rang Lindy and told her I was aboard. By now the shoot date was close and by the time I'd done wardrobe I only had time for two lessons with singing coach Mary Hammond. I started pestering Lindy for the state of the deal.

'Everything is in place but Vanessa's management has grabbed top billing.'

'Is that it?'

'Yes, that's how it stands.'

'You mean that's the only thing in the way.'

'That's right.'

'Listen, Lindy, I have never concerned myself with the billing, it is the part I care about, just agree the deal.'

'Yet yours is the main role.'

'It's not important, let's go ahead.'

On the first day in the studio, camera and costume tests, I ran into Vanessa on the way from our dressing rooms to the set. She gave me her warmest Redgrave smile.

'Oh Terence, my agent tells me he secured top billing for me.'

'It's fine by me.'

'Yes, but you are the lead part...'

'Vanessa, please, you are a great actress. I'm happy for you.'

'Terence, you're a real artist and I want you to have it. I'm going to speak to my agent.'

Vanessa takes very seriously all the parts she accepts, and Marion was no exception. The first day we worked together I hardly recognised her. She had transmuted herself into a woman with a life-threatening condition.

As soon as we were in front of the camera, I experienced a quiet sense of fulfilment. It was a gathering of energy not separate from Vanessa's. We were both of an age when we knew better to acknowledge things of this nature, yet it couldn't have begun better. The director, young and relatively inexperienced, knew what he wanted and printed the initial take. This was to become the norm. As was the rapport between Vanessa and myself. It isn't an exaggeration that this harmonic also reverberated into my scenes with the glamorous, extremely good Gemma Arterton. If the truth be told, on every day I worked, the inner vibration or inner life came over me, I stayed present and open to it. That is, until the final day's shooting when the climactic ballad awaited me.

The day dawned, yet it wasn't until the closing moments of the shoot that everything was prepared and I was called to the set. I knew the lyrics, I knew the melody, the beat. The whole shoot had been the realisation of a long-held wish. I had to trust it.

By the time the lights and camera were in place, it actually was the end of the day. There was only time for one take, possibly two.

As I stood on my mark I guess I was expecting the joyful feeling of otherness as on the previous day. Yet it wasn't. The brain was still, silent, aware yet seemingly helpless. There was nothing to be done. Then I felt a downshift in the rhythm of the breath. Into the pause of thought came a sentence: True presence seems empty yet it is fully present.

The band struck up and I sang my song for Marion. Two cameras. One take. Live sound. OK with the director and troupe.

Curiously it occurred to me that this could be my last film. I didn't give it a lot of airtime, yet it did occur to me. I decided to wait and see what happened.

What happened was it opened really well in London, and the Weinstein brothers, Harvey and Bob, grabbed it for the US.

I was visiting my old chum Herbie Kretzmer, whose life had taken a turn for the better. After writing the English lyrics for Charles Aznavour's 'Yesterday When I was Young' and 'She', he'd been commissioned to pen the English lyrics of *Les Misérables*. He made a lot of cash very quickly. Got married, gave up his penthouse in Lincoln House, Basil Street, and had taken up residence in a tree-filled avenue off Kensington Church Street. He had given up his position at the *Daily Mail* and had been flown to Los Angeles to promote *Les Miz* when it received a handful of Oscar nominations. At an Academy party he'd been introduced to Harvey Weinstein. On hearing that Harvey had secured the US rights for *Song for Marion*, Herbie told him 'Stamp is one of my closest friends'. Harvey looked him in the eye and said: 'You tell him Harvey Weinstein is going to get him a Best Actor Academy nomination, tell him I told you myself.' Herbie couldn't wait to relay the message.

When the film opened in the US, retitled by Harvey as *The Unfinished Song*, the Weinsteins didn't dig too deep to promote it, which nowadays reputedly secures Academy nominations.

Ah, nostalgia for the days when a gentleman's word was his bond. Our heartfelt film died the death. Unfinished Song alright, Harvey!

31

My silent father

It is summer 2013. My manager Beth Holden telephones to tell me she has received an offer for me to play one of the last Cossacks; it will shoot in Kiev, Ukraine. The story is a version of how Stalin exterminated the Ukrainians, what Putin is doing now. 'The film is privately financed; the director has done some reputable dramas for television. They will need you for twelve days. The money is good. They want to know if you can ride a horse. Shall I send you the script?'

As I hadn't been paid much for *Song for Marion*, I turned a positive eye on *The Devil's Harvest*. It was good, my character mostly on horseback. I rang Beth. 'Please make it clear to them I can ride, yet be sure to tell them whilst riding is a lot like riding a bicycle in that you don't forget how to do it, I haven't ridden in a film since Blue. Make sure they understand, OK?' No problem.

The lead would be played by Jeremy Irons' son, Max Irons, as my grandson. When we arrived in Kiev the conflict had reached the city. In fact, the hotel where we were billeted backed onto the square where the fires burned all night.

We left early every morning to film in the surrounding countryside. Swashbuckling sword-bearing Cossacks against rifle-bearing soldiers of Stalin.

On the first day I was introduced to my magnificent white steed, informed he had the habit of lifting his forelegs when brought to a halt: 'Just bring him down, it looks impressive, romantic.' Of course the first time astride my mount and bringing him to a 'romantic' stop, there was no mention of my lack of practice.

On the final day of my equestrian efforts, I had two days left of shooting on foot, I was directed to ride up an incline, bring my steed to a halt on a mark, and play a scene with the actor playing my son, Barry Pepper, which I did. It is worth a mention that a more confident director would have held me on the mark and changed the lens on the camera for a close-up. As it happened, I was asked to return to my start mark while the close-up lens was fitted. I did as instructed, my last set-up in the saddle.

It is timely to report a few facts us would-be Cossacks had not been told, by intention or oversight, it's now impossible to tell. The horses were not what you would call 'film horses', trained in a circus reputedly, and secondly they were not geldings but full stallions. You could say it was the actors' fault for not closely inspecting our steeds' fathering equipment. On the other hand, why ... What I didn't know then that I have been told about since is that stallions are more easily bored than their fellow relatives: they don't like repeating the same thing.

To continue the action: On bringing him to a standstill on his mark, he raised his two forelegs. I gently brought him down, then he reared up completely. I slid backwards over his rump and landed on the grass squarely on my shoulders. No pain. No harm done. However – it's a big however – on looking up I realised the horse itself had lost its balance and was tumbling directly onto me. I am sure you've contributed like me to the idea that one's final thoughts are somehow significant, and in that moment, certain it would be my last, the thought flashed through my mind: 'When the tabloids get hold of this, the headline will be: "Aging movie actor killed by horse's arse".' And then the half a ton of white stallion crashed onto me. If his fall had been twelve inches higher, I wouldn't be here today, yet the full weight was directed onto my chest and pelvis. Under the impact, slightly off-centre to the right, my body instinctively curled in on itself, but that was the direction, against the curve, that he chose to roll off me. Hence the later diagnosis of two torn ribs, a rotator cuff tear, six fractures to the pelvis, and a torn bladder.

In the East End, where I spent my formative years, if you get knocked down you get up or it's likely you'll get kicked silly. Which is what I unthinkingly attempted to do. Barry Pepper, playing my son, a fine actor and a fine man, who witnessed the near-death collision, sprang into action and held me still. He saved me hurting myself more. 'Don't move', he repeated in my ear.

An ambulance was summoned. It took some time to reach us in the countryside. I was inspected, lifted onto a stretcher, and driven to Saint Paul's Hospital, Kiev, where no one spoke English. An English-speaking interpreter from the UN was rushed to my side. She translated the results of the X-rays. The surgeon explained that everything would heal, but the tear in the bladder was bleeding and needed surgery as quickly as possible. The producer was intending to have me flown back to London. Yet it was the surgeon's opinion that the tear should be fixed now.

In a dazed state but feeling no pain, I had a good look at him.

'Can you do this?' I asked.

'I can', he replied.

'Let's do it.'

It didn't occur to me to tell them how my system wasn't accustomed to pills or drugs, and I had no idea how long I was under the anaesthetic. I came to, flat on my back, positioned and strapped so as not to move. As I could only move my arms I continued with my alternative breathing exercises. I was unconscious a lot.

On the tenth day, an ambulance Learjet for one was flown from Hamburg to ferry me to London. The very competent young German attendants prepared me for the trip. A trip it was, too – God only knows what they put into my arm before sealing me up on a portable stretcher and conveying me to the little jet where they affixed my stretcher on to a horizontal space so I could see out of the window. The falling sun was unusually appreciated. On landing at Northolt, the airport Their Majesties fly into, my passport was inspected and I was put in the hands of a London Ambulance Driving Team.

'Ow yer feeling, Tel?' they wanted to know.

'I haven't felt so good since the Sixties', I replied.

Big laugh. 'And this is legal, right?'

They heaved me into the back of their ambulance. I wished my German team all the best. One of my new London pals asked me: 'Are you all right with the siren?'

'Sure. Why?'

'Oh, there's a crash on the circular, with the siren on we can just go with the satnav.' What they really wanted to show me, a fellow Cockney, was that they could give Lewis Hamilton a go on the back streets of the capital. It took them sixteen minutes flat to get me from Northolt to the Princess Grace Clinic at the top of Marylebone High Street.

The Devils producers had been persuaded by the crack London-based surgical team – two: one for pelvis, the other for bladder – that they could get me back to work more speedily than the Kiev team's estimate.

It was decided the pelvic expert would go in through the cut made in my solar plexus by the Kiev surgeon. Yet on examination of the wound it was discovered I had been infected by E.coli in St Paul's. Looking around the magnificent Princess Grace Clinic, I began to realise how ancient the St Paul's had been.

The pinning of the pelvis was put on hold. Then the surgeon, no doubt under pressure from the film's producers, would go in through my back to insert the pins. The afternoon before the procedure, set for 9am the next morning, the anaesthetist came to see me. I remember a beautiful, delightfully considerate woman to whom I explained, asked, not to be given too much gas. She reassured me.

That evening I began to get a pain in my chest. I pressed the buzzer always to hand. Whizzed to the MR chamber, it was revealed a blood clot behind my pelvis, previously unnoticed, had begun to move. The surgeon, in black tie, came to my bedside.

'Too dangerous to operate', he considered.

Apparently on his way back to his evening, he and the lovely anaesthetist ran into each other. He explained the situation.

'He seems really unlucky', he concluded.

'You could see it another way', she surmised. 'Maybe he is only meant to lie still and let his pelvis heal itself.'

Which is precisely what happened. So pin-less I remain. I owe you one, beautiful creature.

It goes without saying that the day I could stand on my feet I was X-rayed and taken to the surgeon's consulting room. He had two images to show me, the first taken the day I arrived from Kiev, the second immediately prior to sitting with him. He drew my attention to the six fractures on arrival. On the current image they were not visible.

'I can't see anything, what's happening?'

'Your body has thrown up a lot of calcium, that's why.'

'But, is that right, OK?'

'Mr Stamp', he began, 'I treated lots of men your age and it takes their bodies months to get where you are in six weeks. I don't know what you're doing, but keep doing it.'

The production from hell put me up at the Berkeley Hotel in Knightsbridge, and although I did everything to beg them to shoot the close-ups in the two days I owed them without flying me back to the spot where my near-death escapade had happened, my pleas fell on ears sealed by budget concerns. Oh yes, I didn't have to mount my feisty steed. Production had fashioned me a wooden horse. But complete the two owed days, I did.

When I say 'near-death' – the breath didn't leave the body. I didn't see hosts of angels. Yet the mind did experience its last moments on this earth. And as the body neared its recovery, the Kiev surgeon's parting words, 'Everything will get better. Yet the bladder may never completely recover, it is one of the most sensitive, delicate organs we possess' proved to be a fact. Nightly my sleep was interrupted every hour, thirty minutes sometimes. After my final return from Kiev post-traumatic stresses began to manifest.

Did I really want to do any more jet flights?

More seriously, did I really want to get up at 5am to complete my exercises to be ready for pick-up at 6am?

Implying, did I love performing as much? Serious, because since I had first set eyes on Gary Cooper, it was a question never before asked. I considered the best blessing, of many in my life, was that I had only earned my living doing the thing I loved.

I decided to convalesce in Ojai. It was still bleak weather in London, and although I didn't relish what jet flights have become, particularly Heathrow, I thought if I can only get there I can work out in water, get some sun, maybe start sleeping better. It was to prove a good move with an unanticipated bonus.

To break up the polar flight to the coast, I had a stopover in New York, where I was a member of the New York Athletic Club: an impressive establishment, not only overlooking Central Park but with unrivalled facilities including a gym, pool and excellent steam bath. Which I availed myself of on arrival. It helps me with jet-lag time difference. I loitered over a solitary supper of Elios and managed to stay up till 9pm, 2am UK time.

As previously mentioned, I frequently have dreams in which my mother appears, but less often my Dad. This night or morning I did have a visit from Tom. In India it is believed that during sleep impressions from the inner world are perceived because the sense of consciousness, which may be called the root of the senses, turn its back, so to speak, on the external world and so begins to see the world within.

I was staying at the Club shooting *Legal Eagles* when my beloved Mum passed away. Yet once again I was back in the place where one chapter ended and another screenplay was on offer.

My Dad's appearance was preceded by his youngest brother Barny, who followed him into the seafaring life along with their Dad. Barny was wearing a singlet, his hair was plentiful and a dark grey. He was in very good nick. When Tom joined us he was stripped for action, topless. How most of his time stoking in the bowels of the ships were spent, no doubt.

His hair was also thick, a tad greyer than his brother, yet his body was ripped. Not one of those 'basement bodies' so plentiful in the movie business where actors try to get in shape quickly for a particular role. No, my father's physique was that of an athlete, the muscles hewn by the regular efforts life brought to their door. He didn't speak but smiled encouragingly.

At Idlewild Airport I was strolling to check in when I saw coming toward me a big man, with another's impressive build. The force of his magnetism drew my look. As he came close he extended his hand.

'You're a great actor', he said slowly.

I took his hand. It was twice the size of my own yet soft, unblemished but strong. The fingers long and sculptured. How many of the planet's strongest fighters had hands as delicate as these, capable of battering opponents into submission, I thought.

'Thank you, sir. But not as great an actor as you are a fighter.'

The smile on his face widened. I was in the magnificent presence of Muhammad Ali.

'Marshalla', I said.

'Al humdu lillah!' he added before wending his way in the other direction.

On the flight to LA I remembered something my youngest brother John had told me. On a vacation to Nassau with our Mum and Dad their plane had stopped to refuel. Passengers had vacated to the airport, he didn't recall which. Getting off another airplane was Muhammad Ali; an impressively tall man, he was surrounded by bodyguards even taller. When they sat down my Dad approached and asked the World Champion for his autograph. Which he charmingly gave. John said he'd been impressed by Tom's request. 'You know how little respect Dad had for most guys.' Indeed I did.

For myself, the fleeting exchange with Muhammad Ali was unusually empowering. Watching him walk away I had thought, all the pain that man has endured fighting and staying fit enough to fight, robbed, by the government, of three of his best years and now judging by the tremors of his elegant hands coping with Parkinson's. It put my injury and recuperation in perspective.

En route to Ojai, I stayed overnight at the Chateau Marmont, my home from home. Their suites have kitchens, a plus for a health food freak like myself, and my glamorous manager Beth Holden came to see me before I travelled to the high desert. I confessed to her my post-traumatic concerns. Women understand these traumas, as they frequently experience them after childbirth. She was sympathetic but didn't buy into my doubts that I might not want to continue acting.

'Why don't we do this', she proposed. 'Let me find you a juicy leading role and you can see how you feel during the actual filming.' I couldn't disagree and, on that note, I made my way up to Ojai.

32

Karma doesn't accept kick-backs

I had recently designed a little house on a piece of land owned by a longtime friend, Richard La Plante. I had provided all the cash, and he and his wife had organised the construction. It hadn't occurred to me to ask for any ownership rights as he'd been a chum for about twenty-five years, but that's another story. The 'guest house' was my dream house. It had a Turkish bath (a steam room) and work-out swimming pool; the whole thing fuelled by solar power.

On my first complete day in Ojai, I drove my Fiat 500E, the best electric vehicle in the world. The powers that be in California reputedly told Mr Fiat that if he didn't build an electric vehicle for the lowest cost they would prohibit all sales of Fiat to California—no such testicles on UK politicians. My destination was the old pepper tree, which, as I approached, I could see was a new angle to how I remembered it.

It transpires that the day after Krishnaji passed over, the ancient tree toppled over. While the trustees were trying to decide how to remove it, the now horizontal trunk of the tree began pushing out new branches. So by the time I came by, the section blocking the road had been trimmed and the main trunk manoeuvred back into its old position.

I gratefully leaned against it, and acknowledging my train of thought, paused it. There was a breeze through the trees and the air in the shade was pleasantly warm.

The image of my Dad and his rejuvenated physique came into my head, followed by something Krishnamurti said of dreams: 'Through constant awareness in the waking hours, the many layers of consciousness yield their contents, their hidden understanding. Then dreams become rarer and their interpretation wider and simpler. As the layers of consciousness are penetrated as they reveal themselves, the state of sleep becomes as important as the wakeful state. Then the awareness of the wakeful hours flows into the awareness of sleep, as that of sleep flows into the awareness of the day.'

Could I assume my own level of awareness was allowing this to come to pass? For sure I felt in the right place at the right time.

A few days later I received a call from the agency in London: Would I be interested in doing a voice-over? It could be recorded in California. I'd be happy to do it but I didn't feel up to the two-hour drive to Hollywood on the motorway, and two hours back. No problem, they'd located a seriously good sound engineer in Ojai.

He was good, too. I was impressed with how he made my voice resonate.

The next day I heard from the trustees of the Ojai Foundation. They were inviting me to record one of Krishnamurti's books for an audio release. Now, I knew that one of the few books that the maestro ever actually put pencil to paper for was *The Notebook*; all other editions were transcribed from recordings of his talks. So, somewhere, I knew the original, inspired, given without notes, in-the-moment delivery, was archived. I had reservations of trying to put myself in the same league. I diplomatically declined. The Foundation persisted. I finally had to face the fact that I was protesting too much. Obviously it wasn't a paying assignment, so when I met Michael Lommel, who was funding the idea from his own pocket, I suggested we use the local sound engineer with the specification that I limit the sessions to one hour per day. Everyone agreed. I prepared by doing nothing except maybe inhaling extra-pure high-desert air. I resisted studying the text of *Commentaries On Living*, only opening the chapter page on 'Action'. Not only did it go silky smooth, but I must confess that the often obscure text was comprehended as I was reading it.

When it was complete, some of the listeners at the Ojai school admitted they had understood things they had missed in the reading of the book. An extra bonus, and a big one, was that Michael Lommel's wife Rowan had been studying breath with long-term students of Krishnamurti's original yoga teacher TKV Desikachar, since she had been a pupil at Brockwood Park and Oak Grove, Ojai. She had continued her studies in India with Desikachar's daughter Mekhala, wife Menaka, and TKV himself. On hearing of my injured problematic bladder, she offered to

Skype Desikachar's son Kausthub and see what he advised.

Within two days I was being instructed in pranayama breathing, designed for me personally to strengthen and re-educate my bladder, accompanied with diagrams for the detailed practices to join me on my return to London.

Within six months of daily devoted practice, the breath had become my religion. As health is more important than anything else on Earth and as health depends entirely upon breath, which is the very life, I consider the breath as of the highest importance. As I write I am sleeping nightly for seven hours without interruption.

The efforts entailed in returning to health have resulted in my becoming fitter than before my near-death experience.

However, the fitness of the body did not include the subtleties of the trauma inflicted on the mind by the near death experience. The opposite. As so often in my life, the opportunity to bring these vagaries into focus manifested in the form of a job: a film of Agatha Christie's only unfilmed missive *The Crooked House*. It was a work that came quite late in her literary career and was initially rejected by her publisher, who thought the conclusion of the mystery unsuitable to her canon. Fortunately for her readers, she advised her publisher to get lost, advising them that she knew more about the construction of a story than they did.

The grey wolf, 25 years sober

The role on offer to me was that of the head of Scotland Yard. It entailed only two weeks' actual shooting for me, but because of the varying locations I would need to keep myself free for six weeks. Of course the production wanted to pay me for the two weeks as opposed to the six.

When I told my old friend Herbert Kretzmer of the impending role he commented, 'Sounds like a waistcoat role to me.' As any advice I get from the great man I take as gospel, at my initial meeting with the designer, Colleen Kelsall at Angel's Costumes, I became partial to a three-piece Fifties whistle, adding I could supply a recently made navy blue Homburg and wear my own shoes.

The half a dozen locations were National Trust estates all within ninety minutes of London, with the exception of Bristol, where I was billeted at the Avon Gorge Hotel with a view of Brunel's masterpiece bridge. The other locations, being within a ninety-minute commute from town, involved being picked up at 5.30am, which meant waking up at 5am to do my yoga before the car arrived.

During my early shooting days I began to experience a new agenda from my inner life: When I was at home I didn't want to go to work, yet when I was actually at work I didn't want to come home. Having one of my monthly telephone catch-ups with my sister-in-law, I mentioned this new phenomenon. She explained – she is a psychic therapist – that it was quite a common occurrence following a 'near-death' experience; observing that when I glanced up and realised the horse was about to crush me, there was an instant when my mind realised this was its final moment on earth. It was the fact. Regardless that the body didn't die or that I made light of it, not suing the production company or getting laughs retelling the story of my final thought: 'When the tabloids hear about my demise the headline will read: "Middle-aged actor killed by horse's arse"'. So what should I do? The symptoms, if that's what they are, are not going away.

'Well first, fully acknowledge the near-death experience. Recognise the post trauma manifestations fully as they occur. And trust your intuition.'

In re-examining the accident, I decided to accept the blame myself. If I had studied my big white steed more carefully I could have counteracted the carelessness of the director and the producers, and realised I was astride a stallion. Stallions, especially those trained for the circus, don't like repetition, get bored easily, all of which I should have known.

The moment I was pronounced fit (for filming) after six weeks on my back in the Princess Grace Clinic, the production enforced their contract and forced me back on the plane to war zone Kiev to complete the two days I owed them, albeit astride a purpose-built wooden horse, for my close-up shots. Probably explaining my reluctance to jet around in the future. An insight did come though. If I could re-connect with a horse, just to say hello, stroke it, perhaps that would be a good place to begin.

The very first experience I had of the countryside was Yalding, the hopfields of Kent where the family went when the annual hop harvest took place. We lived in corrugated iron huts on the common of New Barns Farm and were paid by the bushel of hops we picked. I explain this as the memories that came to me were of a Shire horse named Colonel who pulled the horse-drawn cart that carried the yellow sacks, the labours of the hopping families from the east end of London who picked them, six days a week. We cooked all our meals in the communal 'cook houses' and one of my jobs was to prepare and tend the log fire. Yet the long forgotten recollection that came back to me was of the gentle giant Colonel, who accepted the manifestation of my affection with the slightest of quivers. If I could locate a fellow Shire and spend a little time with him, it might be a start on the road to my post-trauma recovery.

During the shoot of *Crooked House*, I struck up a telephone rapport with the Production Co-ordinator Arabella Gilbert. She immediately responded to the changes in scene rescheduling, as the on-the-floor assistants were often too busy to ring me back. Learning the words and going to bed early are the vagaries of aging performers.

On one such occasion she asked me about the accident: it was rumoured about on set. I finished the tale of woe by explaining my ruse to meet one of the big horses that pull the gun carriages as part of the Household Cavalry Regiment, and who are housed in the Knightsbridge barracks, yet had not come up with a way of approach. 'I may be able to help you with that,' she responded. It transpired her father had been a General. And so it was I found myself, suitably attired, outside the barracks' entrance with Arabella, who would introduce me to Squadron Leader Alexander who would conduct the tour.

I must confess I have always considered the building one of the ugliest constructions to eyesore the skyline of the surrounding Hyde Park. Councils had rejected its design yet it was forced through by Royal influence. However, once inside it was a different story: the ugly twin of the Park Lane Hilton housed treasures Mr Hilton never dreamed of.

When we lived in Plaistow our Mum, between children, worked as a barmaid at the Abbey Arms pub. The evening job helped out the family finances as our Dad only earned £12 a week. Sometimes I would walk with my Mum to the pub, which was located in Barking Road. On the other side of the street, the whole corner of Esk Road was a blacksmiths, where I spent many hours of my boyhood watching the local horses being shod.

These long forgotten times came flooding back on my initial descent into the basement mysteries of the Household Cavalry's tower block, when I was introduced to the farriers fashioning horseshoes amidst their open furnaces.

Next stop: I was taken by Squadron Leader Alexander to meet his horse George, the black steed he rode and exercised. George was a big boy, seventeen hands or so.

I'd heard of a horse whisperer who advised one to get close enough to a strange horse to allow him to inhale your breath. Which I proceeded to do, exhaling fully from the solar plexus area of my tummy. It is believed in the whispering circles that horses catch the essence of a person in their breath. I assumed I passed muster as he reached toward my outstretched hand and proceeded to give it a good lick. When I withdrew my hand he nuzzled my face. 'That's unusual,' Alexander said. 'He's generally wary of strangers.'

Mercury helping me with my recovery

This pattern was repeated when I met one of the trumpeters, equally statuesque white steeds: Wellesley. Nuzzling my face and licking my hands. But finally I was introduced to Mercury, a Shire who hauled one of the gun carriages. Mercury was an unusual colour, a heathered mixture of mid-brown and white. He pushed his majestic head out of his stall as I pronounced his name. I blew my breath toward him, and as he moved his nostrils side to side I coincided my head in unison with his. When I moved close, he nuzzled me in a most welcoming manner.

On reflection of my thrilling day at the barracks, I had the romantic notion that the combined welcoming of George, Wellesley and Mercury was letting me know that their brethren in Kiev meant me no harm.

During my protracted journey to make sense of my association with Krishnamurti, several things all came together seemingly all at once. I guess it was triggered when reading Rumi, when I came across the line:

'In the silence of love can be found the spark of life.'

In the silence of love... It wasn't inferred, it wasn't implied, it was a statement, a fact, by no other than the Shakespeare of Persia, who didn't write plays, didn't couch his great truths in dramatic situations – he wrote poetry. He didn't waste a line, a word. There was no escape. That was Rumi. In the silence of love, the mind is silent, empty, at one with what is, the identical 'What is' of Krishnamurti. The 'What is' when he paused, laid his hands on my arm, and using his presence, in the present, paused the thoughts in my brain and allowed me a moment of silence, the silence of love to be at one with the cloud, the sky, the spark of life that was experience in the What is, from my own standpoint.

He made me aware, for the very first time, of the timeless movement of the alone. That which precedes thought. Always there, yet previously unnoticed. He touched the depth of what Mr Gary Cooper had initially ruffled. Small wonder it had taken all this confusion to arrive at the subtlety of his touch. 'Look at the cloud', indeed. In the silence, in the emptiness; the moment of the alone, then only the journey of the unknowable.

He had encouraged 'what was looking' to surface into my present awareness.

EPILOGUE

Alone – all one?

What can I tell you that I haven't already told you?

Do I get depressed, lonely? Of course. It's not my job to be different, only to see things differently.

When I was approached to scribble this tome, the initial thinking was a way of conveying to young folks driven to an artistic existence what I had learned from artists finer than myself.

What can I tell you that I haven't already told you?

Engage in what life presents. It has its own reasons. Maybe it isn't what you've hoped for. But hope is like honey. Don't indulge in it.

Be present and notice when you're not, this is the root into a heightened state of awareness. Allow it to flow over into your life – any time. It is the cog that only appears to turn; yet its radiant presence is the foundation for all the actions in what we call our body.

Aim high. Life will support you. It is resonating in your own heart. Have faith in it.

The sky is your being, your awareness. Silent, unmoving, yet all movement manifests from it: the luminous peace at your core. Pay attention to that – be at one with that. Now. Just now.

I think that's what my Mum was pointing me toward.

My real home. Your real home. When the seeking ends the thrill begins. Only then the never-ending journey of the unknowable.

Stand by. On your marks. Action!

'You are the teacher, the taught and the teaching. You are the book of life' – K's final few loving words to his colleagues before he passed on.